THE REALLY STUPID THINGS LIBERALS BELIEVE

Daniel Hathaway

Liberals believe many astonishingly stupid things because they tend to believe completely in things in the complete absence, or almost complete absence, of evidence in the presence of overwhelming contradictory evidence. This book is about those things.

Author

Daniel Hathaway

Daniel Hathaway

Printed in the United States of America

First Printing: September 2017

For Mom and Dad

CONTENTS

THE STUPID THINGS
LIBERALS BELIEVE

MODIFIED FOOD
IS HARMFUL TO
PEOPLE AND THE
ENVIRONMENT
4. WHITE MALE
PRIVILEGE
5. FEMINISM IS AN
EQUALITY
MOVEMENT
6. SUGAR IS BETTER
FOR YOU THAN
ARTIFICIAL
SWEETENERS LIKE
ASPARTAME

7. SMOKING MARIJUANA IS HEALTHY

8. THERE IS A WAGE GAP BETWEEN MEN AND WOMEN THAT IS THE RESULT OF DISCRIMINATION

"Life is achievement...Give yourself an aim, something you want to do, then go after it, breaking through everything, with nothing in mind but your aim, all will, all concentration-and get it" ~Ayn Rand

CHAPTER 1

THE REALLY STUPID THINGS LIBERALS BELIEVE: LIBERALS ARE TOLERANT OF OTHER PEOPLE'S BELIEFS

"My hubris is better than your hubris"

For every one Sociologist who does not identify as a liberal, eight other sociologists do. For example, in three separate studies, researchers found that self-identified Democrats outnumber Republicans by ratios of at least 8 to 1. [1] [2] [3] In contrast, some 18 percent of social scientists say they are Marxist. So, it's easier to find a Marxist in the social sciences than it is to find a Republican in the Social Sciences.[4] Sociology, is basically the Liberal, politically correct version of science.

People in the Social Sciences believe things that no other Scientists believe. For example, Sociologists believe the brain is a general purpose cognition device shaped almost entirely by culture. [5] [6] However, studies in subjects like Molecular Biology, Genetics, Evolutionary Psychology, Neuroscience, Economics et cetera contradict this claim.

Out of all the disciplines that contradict Sociology the most, Evolutionary Psychology is probably the discipline most diametrically opposed to Sociology. Evolutionary psychologists argue that much of human behavior is the result of psychological adaptations that evolved to solve recurrent problems in human ancestral environments.[7] Evolutionary Psychologists and other Scientists believe the mind may, at least in part, be composed of innate neural structures or modules which have distinct established evolutionarily developed functions. Evolutionary psychologists hold that behaviors or traits that occur universally in all cultures are good candidates for evolutionary adaptations.[8]   Some Cultural universals include behaviors related to language, cognition, social roles, technology, and gender roles.[9]

For example, in contrast to Evolutionary Psychology, Social Scientists believe behaviors related to language, cognition, social roles, technology, and gender roles are all cultural constructs, according to their, "standard social science model." The standard social science model is sometimes called the "blank slate", "relativist", "social constructionist", and "cultural determinist" perspective that assumes the mind is shaped almost entirely by culture.[10]

Judith Lorber is a Professor Emerita of Sociology and Women's Studies at The CUNY Graduate Center and Brooklyn College of the City University of New York who is reputed to have, "made a significant contribution to gender studies," by writing a book, that has become a "bible,"   and "mandatory reading," in Women's Studies classes.[11][12] Lorber's Book, "Paradoxes of Gender," published by Yale in 1994, contends,

---

...sex, sexuality, and gender are all socially constructed. [13] Bodies differ in many ways physiologically; but they are completely transformed by social practices to fit into the salient categories of a society, the most pervasive of which are 'female' and 'male and 'women' and 'men'." [13]

Lorber argues that men's and women's brains differ physiologically, but this physiological difference does not determine Gender. According to Lorber, culture determines Gender, not Anatomy, not Physiology. However, Scientists in other disciplines like Biology, Neuroscience, and Biochemistry have determined that form follows function, and function dictates form. In other words, Physiology determines Anatomy and Anatomy determines Physiology. Furthermore, Biologists, Neuroscientists, and Biochemists have determined that the Anatomy of Men's and women's brains are different, therefore, their Physiology is different and since their Physiology is different, their gender is also different.

For instance, take one module in the brain, the hypothalamus. The size of the hypothalamus tends to be larger in men than it is in women, [14] and that's not the only difference. Several hypothalamic nuclei are sexually dimorphic as well; i.e., there are clear differences in the structure of hypothalamic nuclei between males and females. Moreover, the importance of these changes can be recognized by Physiological aka Functional differences between males and females. For instance, males of most species prefer the odor and appearance of females over males, which is instrumental in stimulating male sexual behavior. Furthermore, the hypothalamus secretes certain neurohormones, called releasing hormones or hypothalamic hormones, and these in turn stimulate or inhibit the secretion of pituitary hormones and one of these hormones is Testosterone.

On average, in adult males, levels of testosterone are about 7–8 times as great as in adult females.[15] *As the metabolic consumption of testosterone in males is greater, the daily production is about 20 times greater in men.*[16][17] *Physiologically, men's levels of testosterone, are known to affect men's mating, risk taking, fathering, aggressive and competitive behavior.*

For example, Fatherhood has been found to decreases testosterone levels in men, suggesting that the resulting emotional and behavioral changes promote paternal care.[18] *When testosterone levels are reduced, then there is more empathy by the father than in fathers whose levels go up.*[19] *Studies have also found that testosterone facilitates aggression by modulating receptors in the hypothalamus and testosterone is significantly correlated with competitive behavior.* [20] *So, by examining just one module in the brain, the hypothalamus, we can see how a difference in the* anatomy of men's and women's brains changes physiology and therefore, also gender.

If Sociologists are right and the mind is a general purpose cognition device shaped almost entirely by culture then how do Sociologists explain how remarkably conserved gender is across disparate cultures? Why do men have higher motivations to take risks, attain social status, and demonstrate athletic prowess in the Netherlands but also in Brazil, Japan, the United States and every other country in the world? [21]

How do Sociologists explain that anthropological studies of a variety of different cultures found women tend to prefer men with higher social status? For example, in hunter gatherer societies the best hunters tend to attract more than their fair share of female sexual selection. They may have two to three times as many offspring. In pastoral cultures the men who have the largest herds of animals attract the most women. In agricultural societies the men *who have the most land, wealth, and military power attract the most women.* [21] *If you disagree, and don't believe that women tend to select men with higher social status, how do you explain why Rock Stars tend to have groupies, and not Garbage men?*

Human culture has been dominated by males because human culture is mostly courtship effort, and all male animals invest more energy in courtship. Male humans paint more pictures, record more jazz albums, and write more books et cetera. And it's not just men who tend to be more prolific than women. In the wild, male nightingales sing more and male peacocks display more impressive visual ornaments. [21]

How do Sociologists explain the number of studies in Molecular Biology examining Y-chromosomal and Mitochondrial DNA that have found throughout human history many more women have reproduced than men? For example, one study examined the Y chromosomal and mitochondrial DNA of 450

Volunteers from 7 world regions and determined that 8,000 years ago 17 women reproduced for every one man. [22] *The researchers in this study believe the reason only 1 man reproduced for every 17 women 8,000 years ago is that only a few men accumulated lots of wealth and power. In other words, men with status reproduced, while men without status did not reproduce.*

Moreover, since 450 volunteers from 7 world regions were used in this study, this is an example of 'universality.' The definition of universality is things done by all people throughout the world with few exceptions. Therefore according to evolutionary psychology women selecting, 'wealthy and powerful,' men as mates is most likely an evolutionary adaptation, rather than as sociologists believe, a cultural construct.

Sociologists argue, yeah but what about Transgender people? Transgender women have the brains of men, but identify as women-right?

Therefore, culture must determine gender, not biology?

This is a good example of what many liberals do when you get in a debate with them. You'll state a rule and liberals will cite an exception to that rule, and the axiom that there are exceptions to every rule is correct. There are exceptions to every rule. For example, there was even a Nazi who saved Jews, Oschar Schindler. Oschar Schindler saved thousands of Jews. However that does not mean Nazis saved Jews, with the exception of Oschar Schindler. Another example is, 1+1 doesn't even always equal 2, in Boolean algebra 1 + 1 = 10. However, that does not mean 1 + 1 = 10, except in Boolean algebra. In other words, there are exceptions to every rule. However, that does not mean the exception invalidates the rule.

It's been proven by scientists across many disciplines that the anatomy and Physiology of men's and women's brains differ, and therefore, so *does their gender. Neuroscientists have even discovered that the brains of transgender women often more closely resemble the brains of the gender they identify with than they do the brains of their birth gender. For example, in one study, transgender women like other women, where found to have fewer cells associa*ted with the regulatory hormone somatostatin than men. In another study, scientists from Spain conducted brain scans on transgender men and found that their white matter was neither typically male nor typically female, but somewhere in between. [23] Therefore, even Transgender people's brains show how Anatomy and physiology determines gender.

One of the clearest examples of how anatomy and physiology underlies many elements of masculinity is a rare genetic condition called androgen insensitivity syndrome. Geneticists discovered babies with androgen insensitivity are born with a Y chromosome and therefore are biologically male, but their bodies cannot process testosterone and so default to the female phenotype. They have features and traits of a woman, smooth hairless skin, minimal body odor, a rudimentary vagina, and they feel themselves to be a woman. [24]

If Gender is a social construct and not innate, then why do so few women graduate with STEM (Science, Technology, Engineering and Math) degrees, only 6.7% of women graduate with STEM degrees. [25] Why do so few women graduate with STEM degrees. Are women discriminated against in STEM Fields, as Sociologists contend? Studies by Economists dispute this claim. For example, for decades, Liberals have claimed that discrimination blocks women from landing academic positions in STEM fields. However a paper published online by the National Academy of Sciences by Wendy M Williams and Stephen J. Cecil titled National Hiring experiments Reveal 2:1 Faculty Preference For Women on STEM Tenure Track found that in experiments with professors from 371 colleges and universities across the United States that science and engineering faculty actually preferred women two-to-one over identically qualified male candidates for assistant professor positions. [26]

If you're preferred 2:1, you're not being discriminated against. Some people might even suggest a 1:1 preference of identically qualified candidates would be equality and a 2:1 preference for women over identically qualified male candidates is actually an indication of discrimination against men, not women. If it's not discrimination that prevents women from studying STEM, then could it be that men's and women's brains are different and therefore tend to be suited for different tasks? Studies going back decades have found males do better on mental tasks involving visual spatial tasks like rotating an object in space, and spatial ability is an ability necessary for success in STEM fields? [27]

Moreover, numerous studies have found the standard deviation of men's intelligence is greater than the standard deviation of women's intelligence, while there is no difference between the mean or average intelligence of men and women. [28] [29] [30] [31] Standard Deviation is the average amount that the trials in a study differ from the mean. In this case, each individual taking an intelligence test is a trial. Therefore, there are more men than women in the top and bottom of the IQ distribution. In other words, there are more intellectually challenged men and more men who are geniuses. So, there are more men capable of getting a degree in STEM than there are women capable of getting a degree in STEM. Therefore, it's not discrimination preventing women from getting a degree in STEM. It is that there are more men capable of getting a degree in STEM.

Females are not only not being discriminated against in STEM. Females are being pushed into studying STEM. For example, an article in the National Geographic titled an "American Girl" by Tina Roseburg found that girls felt pressure from adults and other girls to excel in science, technology, engineering and math. One fifteen year old girl remarked in her article, "STEM was very hard for me."[32]

Furthermore, Sociologists cannot explain the higher male motivations to take risks, attain social status, and demonstrate athletic prowess. [21] Most Sociologists contend the reason only 18% of the worlds firms have a female as top chief executive officer and only 2% of the world's 500 biggest companies are headed by a female CEO is discrimination, yet sociologists are unable to explain why men work so much harder than women. Men are much more likely to work more over time hours and women are much more likely to work part time. [33] In other words, men tend to work harder than women.

Men work harder because they are more motivated to attain social status in order to be attractive to women. The reason so many more men than women are CEO's of fortune 500 companies[32] is because men have a higher incentive to attract large numbers of sexual partners while, on the other hand, women are motivated to mate with men with the highest social status. It's the same in nature. Females of several bird species such as blackbirds, nightingales, sedges, warblers, mockingbirds, parrots and mynahs have been found to prefer males who display larger song repertoires, with greater diversity and novelty[21] In other words, female human beings and female birds are both attracted to status but in a female birds mind status is determined by the male birds song repertoire but in humans, it's determined by a man's position and wealth.

So why do Sociologists believe such dumb things? Why do Sociologists believe completely in things in almost the complete absence of evidence, in the presence of overwhelming contradictory evidence? A study titled, Political Diversity Will Improve Social Psychological Science, by Duert et al, (2014) found a possible reason why Sociologists believe such stupid things. The researchers in this study found that there is an "underrepresentation of non-liberals in social psychology [that] is most likely due to a combination of self-selection, hostile climate, and discrimination." [34] They found, "ample evidence using multiple methods demonstrating that social psychologists do in fact act in discriminatory ways toward non-liberal colleagues and their research. " [34]

For example, in a study titled, *Human subjects review, personal values, and the regulation of social science research*, (1985) researchers conducted an experiment in which Research proposals hypothesizing either "reverse discrimination" (i.e., against White males) or conventional discrimination (i.e., against ethnic minorities) were submitted to 150 Internal Review Boards. Everything else about the proposals was held constant. The "reverse discrimination" proposals were approved less often than the conventional discrimination proposals. [35]In another study by Inbar, Y., & Lammers, J. (2012) titled, *Political diversity in social and personality psychology*, found that 82% of social psychologists who responded to a survey admitted to being willing to discriminate against conservatives. [36]

In another study by, Abramowitz, Gomes, & Abramowitz, (1975) titled, *Publish or politic: Referee bias in manuscript review and another study* by Ceci, Peters, & Plotkin, (1985) titled, *Human subjects review, personal values, and the regulation of social science research*, found that in peer review, confirmation biases lead reviewers to work extra hard to find flaws with papers whose conclusions they disliked, while being more permissive about methodological issues when they endorsed the conclusions of a study [35] [37]

Therefore we can see why sociologists believe such ridiculous things. They are biased. Rarely does anything come from sociology that upsets liberal sensibilities. If the conclusions of a study are not politically correct then liberal sociologists will censor that study during peer review. Political Correctness works as de facto liberal censorship in Sociology. For example, Hardin & Higgins, (1996) found that Sociologists have a shared reality that subsequently blinds its members to morally or ideologically undesirable hypotheses and unanswered but important scientific questions. [38]

When there is anti-intellectualism, like censoring ideas based on political ideology, such as discriminating against conservatives in social psychology, liberal values and assumptions can become embedded into theory and method and what is subjective ostensibly becomes objective. For example, social psychology researchers claim anyone who disagrees with their research as being in, "denial," and even further they claim that their findings are, "reality." That is their findings are, "facts." [34]

Sociologists believe stupid things because for every sociologist who is not a liberal eight others are and they have a liberal skewed confirmation bias. Conformation Bias is when people search for evidence that will confirm their existing beliefs while also ignoring or downplaying disconfirming evidence.

Scientists in other fields have worked out a lot of how the mind works. For example, Neuroscientists know a lot about how the modules of the mind work. Neuroscientists know large modules in the brain coordinate inputs from smaller brain modules which collate inputs from even smaller brain modules and they have even discovered that this reduction continues all the way down to single neurons. In some cases, neuroscientists even know exactly which neuron responds to which stimulus. For example, large brain modules such as the cortex coordinate inputs from smaller brain modules such as the temporal lobes, which collate neural events from even smaller brain modules like the angular gyrus and this reduction continues all the way down to a single neuron. Incredibly, neuroscientists working with neurosurgeons have even found the single neuron that fires when the subject is shown a photograph of Bill Clinton. However, sociologists ignore the evidence that the brain consists of modules that evolved to solve problems in our prehistoric past and instead believe the brain is nothing more than a general purpose cognition device shaped entirely by culture.

In general, Liberals tend to believe completely in things in almost the complete absence of evidence, in the presence of overwhelming contradictory evidence. In this case the overwhelming contradictory evidence comes from the consensus of a multitude of other disciplines like, Molecular Biology, Genetics, Evolutionary Psychology, Neuroscience, and Economics.

Liberals pride themselves on their tolerance of other people's beliefs, and they are very tolerant of other people's beliefs, as long as those people believe the same things they do. In other words, Liberals are not tolerant of other people's beliefs at all.

Chapter 2

THE STUPID THINGS
LIBERALS BELIEVE
ALTERNATIVE
MEDICINE: LIBERALS
ARE SUSPICIOUS OF
MAINSTREAM
MEDICINE BUT THEY
ENTHUSIASTICALLY
EMBRACE ALTERNATIVE
MEDICINE WITHOUT
QUESTION.

"S.C.A.M (Supplementary, Complementary and Alternative Medicine)"

Alternative medicine is another example of a stupid thing liberals believe because they believe completely that it works in almost the complete absence of any evidence that it works in the presence of overwhelming contradictory evidence that it does not work.

Alternative medicine includes practices claimed to have the healing effects of medicine but which are disproven, unproven, impossible to prove, or are excessively harmful in relation to their effect; and where the scientific consensus is that the therapy does not, or cannot, work because the known laws of nature are violated by its basic claims.

On the other hand, mainstream medicine is, 'evidence based' medicine. 'Evidence-based medicine (EBM) is the application of the scientific method to medicine. This is done by applying modern scientific and statistical methods, to help make rational decisions for individual patients, based on the available evidence and our existing body of knowledge. Researchers in Evidence-based medicine, try to disprove hypotheses, in contrast, biased researchers in alternative medicine often strive to confirm pre-existing notions, which is not science. It's 'pseudoscience'.[39] Pseudoscience is a belief that is incorrectly presented as scientific. In simpler terms, pseudoscience is fake evidence.

Alternative medicine in the west began to rise following the counterculture movement of the 1960s, as part of the rising new age movement of the 1970s.[40][41][42] This was due to misleading mass marketing of "alternative medicine" being an effective "alternative" to biomedicine, changing social attitudes about not using chemicals and challenging the establishment and authority of any kind, and sensitivity to giving equal measure to beliefs and practices of other cultures.[43][44][45][46][47][48][49]

Despite being disproven, unproven, or impossible to prove, the 'NCCIH' (the Federal Government's lead agency for scientific research on complementary and integrative health approaches) states that more than 30 percent of adults and about 12 percent of children in America use health care approaches developed outside of mainstream Western, or conventional, medicine. [50] Furthermore, according to the national science foundation's biennial report (April 2002), titled, *"The state of science understanding,"* 88 percent [of people] agree that alternative medicine is a viable means of treating illness. Moreover, according to the American Medical Association, the number of visits to alternative practitioners exceeds visits to traditional medical doctors. Many of these approaches are benign. Benign treatments have the advantage of not directly injuring a patient, other than money and at worst precious time going out the window, however; some of them are down-right harmful, such as, say, drilling a hole in the skull to let in more oxygen," [47]

There are several psychological issues that are critical to the growth of alternative medicine. One of the most critical is the placebo effect – a well-established observation in medicine.[49] The placebo effect is a psychological phenomenon, in which the recipient perceives an improvement in a condition due to personal expectations, rather than the treatment itself. Related to the, placebo effect there are several cognitive biases such as, the, 'regression fallacy,' (assuming that something has returned to normal because of corrective actions taken while it was abnormal, where improvement that would have occurred anyway is credited to alternative therapies. This fallacy fails to account for natural fluctuations.) 'confirmation biases,' 'pattern recognition,' (finding patterns where none exist,) the *post hoc, ergo propter hoc* fallacy(correlation does not always equal causation), and the power of suggestion. These cognitive biases have contributed to the growth of Alternative Medicine.[50]

An interesting example of how, 'the power of suggestion,' has contributed to the growth of alternative medicine is an experiment by Benjamin Franklin and Antoine Lavoisier in 1784 to test the claims of a German physician, Franz Anton Mesmer. Mesmer claimed that just as an invisible force of magnetism draws iron shavings to a lodestone, the same invisible force flows through living beings, blockage of which causes disease. Mesmer claimed the cure for the disease comes through releasing the blockage using magnets. To test the null hypothesis that magnetism had no effect and was all in the mind, Franklin and Lavoisier, deceived some subjects into thinking they were receiving the experimental treatment when they were not, while others did receive the treatment but were told they had not. The results were clear. Those subjects who thought they had received the treatment but had not, believed they were cured. While those who actually received the treatment but were told they had not believed there was no effect. In other words, Mesmer's results were nothing more than the 'power of suggestion.'

Today we know that iron atoms in a magnet are crammed together in a solid state about one atom apart from each other. While, in the blood only four iron atoms are allocated to each hemoglobin molecule and they are separated by distances too great to form a magnet. However, to this day, people believe in, 'bio-magnetic therapy,' and Americans spend about 300 million dollars a year on magnets believing they have a powerful healing effect on the body.

Sometimes an alternative medicine supporter will present a scholarly work as "evidence" that the alternative medicine works and is being suppressed by "regular" medicine. The problem is the work is either outdated, has been refuted by later research, or (worse) is misrepresented. In other words, the proponents of alternative medicine use confirmation bias. Confirmation bias is the tendency to search for, interpret, favor, and recall information in a way that confirms one's preexisting beliefs or hypotheses. People display this bias when they gather or remember information selectively, or when they interpret it in a biased way. For example, the proponents of alternative medicine cite selective portions of a study on a meta-analysis of Homoeopathy by K. Linde, N. Clausius, G. Ramirez, et al., titled, *"Are the� Clinical Effects of Homoeopathy Placebo Effects? A Meta-analysis of Placebo-Controlled Trials,"* in the *Lancet*, September 20, 1997, [51] portions of which seem to prove homeopathy works, while proponents of alternative medicine ignore later studies that refute homeopathy. For example, in a later study, titled,

"The end of homoeopathy" *The Lancet*, looked at 14 studies from 2003 to 2007 and found that homoeopathy has no proven clinical benefits. [52] Moreover, contrary to the popular belief that alternative treatments are being 'suppressed', significant expense is paid to test alternative medicine, including over $2.5 billion spent by the United States government over 17 years as of 2009, and almost none show any effect beyond that of false treatment. [53]

Obviously, if 2.5 billion dollars has been spent studying alternative medicine, then alternative treatments are not being, 'suppressed,' by mainstream medicine. For example, $374,000 was spent finding that inhaling lemon and lavender scents does not promote wound healing; $750,000 was spent to find that prayer does not cure AIDS or hasten recovery from breast-reconstruction surgery; $390,000 was spent to find that ancient Indian remedies do not control type 2 diabetes; $700,000 was spent to find that magnets do not treat arthritis, carpal tunnel syndrome, or migraine headaches; and $406,000 was spent to find that coffee enemas do not cure pancreatic cancer."[54]

Alternative Medicine practitioners often cite successful treatments of transitory or ephemeral illnesses that go away on their own as a result of the body's immune system healing itself, which would have happened anyway regardless of any alternative medical treatments that had been used. For example, a transitory illnesses such as, say, a common cold going away after taking an alternative remedy. This is an example of the, 'post hoc, ergo propter hoc fallacy.' The, 'post hoc, ergo propter hoc fallacy,' is a logical fallacy that states "Since event Y *followed* event X, event Y must have been *caused* by event X. For example, a post hoc, ergo propter hoc fallacy could be claiming, 'rooster's crow immediately before sunrise, therefore; roosters must cause the sun to rise'. In other words, correlation does not equal causation. Just because someone got better after using an alternative medical treatment doesn't mean the alternative medical treatment is what healed them. But human beings are masters at finding patterns in things where no pattern exists, which is known as pattern recognition.

We are pattern seeking animals after all. We're the descendants of hominids who were especially good at making causal connections between events in nature. The associations were real often enough that the process became ingrained in our neural anatomy and physiology. Unfortunately, our proclivity for making causal relationships between things also results in identifying false patterns where no causal relationship exists. The solution to identifying real causal relationships from false causal relationships is science.

The Oxford Dictionary defines the scientific method as "a method or procedure that has characterized natural science since the 17th century, consisting in systematic observation, measurement, and experiment, and the formulation, testing, and modification of hypotheses." [55] The overall method involves making falsifiable hypotheses based on observations, deriving predictions from those hypotheses as logical consequences, and then carrying out experiments to test those predictions to determine whether the original hypothesis was correct.[56] Then the results of those experiments are confirmed by being reproduced by a group of the original researcher's peers, in a process known as, "peer review." In general, the strongest tests of hypotheses come from carefully controlled and replicated experiments that gather, "empirical" data or data based on, observation or experience rather than theory or pure logic. Depending on how well the results of experiments match the predictions, the original hypothesis may require refinement, alteration, expansion or even rejection.

The vaccine used to treat smallpox is an excellent example of how the Scientific Method has been used to create an effective medicine that led to the complete eradication of a disease. Smallpox is believed to have been acquired by humans from a terrestrial African rodent between 16,000 and 68,000 years ago, well before the dawn of agriculture and civilization. The disease killed an estimated 400,000 Europeans annually during the closing years of the 18th century [57] and was responsible for a third of all blindness.[58][59] However, as a result of vaccination campaigns during the 19th and 20th centuries, using a vaccine created using the scientific method, the World Health Organization certified the global eradication of smallpox in 1980.[60]

Noting the common observation that milkmaids were generally immune to smallpox, a physician Edward Jenner postulated that the pus in the blisters that milkmaids received from cowpox (a disease similar to smallpox, but much less virulent) protected them from smallpox. In other words, using the scientific method, Jenner made an observation, milkmaids were generally immune to smallpox and from this observation, he created a hypothesis, "The pus in the blisters that milkmaids received from cowpox protected them from small pox."

Furthermore, using the scientific method, Jenner devised a way of testing his hypothesis by performing an experiment based on this prediction. Jenner's hypothesis theorized that inoculating someone with cowpox would result in them acquiring immunity to smallpox. Jenner inoculated a boy with cowpox blisters he had acquired by scraping pus from cowpox blisters from the hands of a milkmaid who had caught cowpox from a cow. [61] Jenner then inoculated the boy in both arms, subsequently producing in the boy a fever and some uneasiness, but no full-blown infection. Later, he injected the boy with material from the small pox virus, the routine method of immunization at that time and no disease followed. The boy was later challenged with more material from the smallpox virus and again the boy showed no sign of infection. Therefore, Jenner proved his hypothesis was correct. Inoculating people with cowpox would result in them acquiring immunity to small pox. [62] Jenner's results were then confirmed by The Royal College of Physicians who reproduced his results. In other words, Jenner's results were confirmed by "peer review." [63]

In contrast, to a medicine discovered using the scientific method like the smallpox vaccine let us examine, homeopathy, an alternative medical treatment. Homeopathy is a system of medical practice that treats a disease especially by the administration of minute doses of a remedy that would in larger amounts produce in healthy persons symptoms similar to those of the disease. Homeopathy was created in 1796 by Samuel Hahnemann, based on his doctrine of *like cures like,* a claim that a substance that causes the symptoms of a disease in healthy people would cure similar symptoms in sick people.[64]

Alternative medicine proponents claim, "one of the ways homeopathy works is by helping to balance your body's energy, or chi as it's called in traditional Chinese medicine." Moreover, they claim, "this energy is circulated through your body along specific meridians, and when this circulation gets disrupted -- illness can result." They even claim this can be, tested using, 'electrodermal screening'. [65]

Electrodermal screening uses devices that alternative medicine proponents claim help to diagnose an illness and thereby, select an appropriate treatment. Proponents claim they work by detecting the, "energy imbalance," causing the problem. Proponents claim the devices can detect whether someone is allergic or sensitive to foods, deficient in vitamins, or has defective teeth. Some claim they can even tell whether a disease, such as cancer or AIDS, is not present. [66]

However, according to Stephen Barret, M. D. of, "quackwatch," these devices, "are used to diagnose nonexistent health problems, select inappropriate treatments, and defraud insurance companies. He says, "the practitioners who use electro-dermal testing are either delusional, dishonest, or both. These devices should be confiscated and the practitioners who use them should be prosecuted." [66]

Using the scientific method, by creating a falsifiable hypothesis based on observations then creating an experiment based on predictions derived from that hypothesis, British researchers, conducted a double-blind study, comparing its results with a Vegatest, device [an electro dermal screening device] to those of conventional skin-prick testing in 30 volunteers, half of whom had previously reacted positively for allergy to cat dander or house dust mite. Each participant was tested with 6 items by each of 3 operators in 3 separate sessions, a total of 54 tests per participant. The researchers concluded that Vegatesting does not correlate with skin prick testing and so should not be used to diagnose these allergies. The authors estimated that more than 500 EDS devices were being used in the United Kingdom to assess sensitivity to potential allergens [67] The Australian College of Allergy has concluded that "Vega testing is a technique of diagnosis without scientific basis." [68] In other words, electrodermal testing is not based on science. It's pseudoscience.

Another way proponents of alternative medicine claim you can determine whether a homeopathic remedy works is by stopping treatment. This is based on the theory that feeling worse after taking a homeopathic remedy is actually a sign that it is working. Dr LaValley a homeopathic practitoner writes,

---

"Feeling worse is actually a sign that the solution is doing its job. It's known as a "healing reaction." He goes on to claim, "The healing reaction occurs because as your body's energy gets stabilized, the buildup of what's known as deposition products -- which is your body's way of trying to "seal" off an active disease state so it can't continue to cause problems -- become mobilized. As they circulate through your system, they provoke an inflammatory response that can make you feel sick or in pain." Therefore, you can determine whether a homeopathic remedy is working by discontinuing to take it because you will know, "If it's a healing response," Dr. LaValley writes, "you would predict that worsening, that inflammatory exacerbation will resolve [upon stopping the treatment]. If in fact it's not a healing response, and they're just having a bad day ... and they continue to feel worse, then it was probably their illness that was causing their symptoms and not the healing response."[65]

In other words, the hypothesis that homeopathic treatments work by triggering, 'a healing response,' is not falsifiable. In order to be scientific, a hypothesis has to be falsifiable. A hypothesis is falsifiable if it is possible to conceive of an observation or an argument which negates it. However, according to proponents of alternative medicine, like Dr. LaValley, if you stop taking a homeopathic remedy and feel better it is evidence that it's a healing response [as a result of the homeopathic remedy]. However, if you feel worse, then it's the result of your illness making you feel sick all along, not the homeopathic remedy. Therefore, either, way there's no way of conceiving of an argument that homeopathic remedies don't work by triggering, 'a healing response' because either you get better as a result of the homeopathic remedy or you are sick as a result of the illness, not the homeopathic remedy. In other words, the hypothesis that homeopathic remedies work is not falsifiable, and therefore not scientific.

One thing for certain is homeopathic remedies are not going to cure your illness or cause symptoms of an illness unless your illness is dehydration and the illness you're suffering from is acute water intoxication because homeopathic remedies are nothing more than very expensive water. Homeopathic remedies are manufactured using a process practitioners call, 'homeopathic dilution, in which a chosen substance is repeatedly diluted in alcohol or distilled water, each time with the containing vessel being bashed against an elastic material, (commonly a leather-bound book).[64] Dilution typically continues well past the point where no molecules of the original substance remain.[67] In other words, homeopathic remedies are diluted so much that none of the active ingredient remains. Even the original creator of homeopathic remedies, Samuel Hahnemann, knew the dilutions he advocated for reduced the concentration of the active substance to such infinitesimal levels that none of the active ingredient was left. However, he believed that the *healing power* of the substance could be preserved and actually concentrated by a process called, 'dynamization'.

Dynamization is conceived as the process of increasing the potency of a substance by progressive dilution, combined with succussion (liquids) or trituration (solids). Homeopathists believe that succussion releases the, "spirit-like," healing essence of the substance and concentrates it, while the dilution removes the physical presence of the substance itself. Thus at a dilution of 30C (30 successive dilutions of 1:100, 1 part active ingredient to 100 parts water) no molecules of the original substance remain; however, homeopathic practitioners claim the potency of the preparation is perceived to be high because at 30C the substance has been extensively, 'dynamized'. [64]

However, homeopathic remedies were created prior to discovery of the basic principles of chemistry, which have proven that homeopathic remedies contain nothing but water. In other words the claims made by homeopathic practitioners violate the basic known laws of nature [69] Homeopathy was developed before knowledge of atoms and molecules, or of basic chemistry, which shows that repeated dilution as practiced in homeopathy produces only water, and that homeopathy is not scientifically valid.[70][71][72][73] Despite, the overwhelming scientific consensus that Homeopathic preparations are not effective for treating any condition; eg, Tuomela, R *(1987); Smith K (2012); Baran GR, Kiana MF, Ladyman J (2013); Samuel SP (2014)*[74] [75] [76] [77]*; and alternative therapies* lack the requisite scientific validation, and their effectiveness is either unproved or disproved.[78][79][80][82]   The use of alternative medicine in the US has increased,[78][83] with a 50 percent increase in expenditures and a 25 percent increase in the use of alternative therapies between 1990 and 1997 in America.[83] Therefore, despite the overwhelming scientific consensus that alternative medical therapies do not work, liberals (mostly liberals) continue to use them.

Chapter 3

THE STUPID THINGS LIBERALS BELIEVE: GENETICALLY MODIFIED FOOD IS HARMFUL TO PEOPLE AND THE ENVIRONMENT.

"Liberal opponents of Genetically Modified Organisms warn that eventually human beings will be genetically modified. But their warnings are little late because genetically modified humans have been in existence for well over a decade. It's called 'gene therapy' and it's saved the lives of many people who would have otherwise died"

Opponents of GMOs are predominantly liberal[84] and they claim that GMO's cause certain illnesses such as Organ Failure, tumor development, cancer, infertility, immune system dysfunction, and even death [85*] They make these claims despite the overwhelming scientific consensus that GMO's are not dangerous. Consensus including the major scientific societies, such as the National Academy of Sciences and the World Health Organization, which have concluded that genetically modified crops are not inherently riskier to human health than conventional food[86,87,88,89,90,91,92] They also claim that GMO production has adverse environmental impacts, that it's inherently unnatural, and that for-profit GM0 food companies (notably Monsanto) are screwing farmers.[84] They make these claims in almost the complete absence of evidence, in the presence of overwhelming contradictory evidence. That's why the belief that genetically modified food is harmful is another one of the stupid thing liberals believe.

Genetically modified organisms are not, "inherently unnatural." Nature has been creating genetically modified organisms long before Researchers ever produced the first genetically modified organism in a lab. Studies have found [93] [94] in a process called, horizontal gene transfer, that genes have been transferred between species in nature without human intervention since the beginning of life. For example in an early study in the 1980's a researcher (Syvanen, 1985) postulated that horizontal gene transfer was involved in shaping evolutionary history from the beginning of life on Earth[95]

Genetically modified foods or GM foods, also known as genetically engineered foods or bioengineered foods, are foods produced from organisms that have had changes introduced into their DNA using the methods of genetic engineering. While, Horizontal gene transfer [84][85] is the movement of genetic material between organisms other than by the ("vertical") transmission of DNA from parent to offspring.[87] Genetic engineering and horizontal gene transfer are so alike that genetic engineering has even been called, "artificial horizontal gene transfer".

For example, the same mechanisms that transfer genes between species in recombinant DNA technology are also thought to be the same mechanisms that genes are transferred between species in nature through Horizontal Gene transfer. For example, the mechanisms: Transformation, Transduction, and bacterial conjugation are thought to be the mechanisms by which genes are transferred between species in nature through horizontal gene transfer and it's these exact same mechanisms that researchers use to create genetically modified organisms in the lab.

For example, transformation, is the genetic alteration of a cell resulting from the introduction, uptake and expression of foreign genetic material (DNA or RNA).[96] Transformation is often used in laboratories to create genetically modified organisms with novel genes into bacteria for experiments or for industrial or medical applications and horizontal gene transfer also occurs by Transduction. In nature, transduction is the process by which bacterial DNA is moved from one bacterium to another by a virus.[96] Furthermore, in nature bacterial conjugation, is a process that involves the transfer of DNA via a plasmid from a donor cell to a recombinant recipient cell during cell-to-cell contact,[96] and This process is also used in genetic engineering to move genes from one species to another species.

Genetic engineering is a set of technologies used to change the genetic makeup of cells, including the transfer of genes within and across species boundaries to produce improved or novel organisms, and the same thing happens in nature with, Horizontal Gene Transfer. Take just one study, on horizontal gene transfer, 'Contribution of Horizontal Gene Transfer to the Evolution of Saccharomyces cerevisiae' [97]

'Contribution of Horizontal Gene Transfer to the Evolution of Saccharomyces cerevisiae' is a study on horizontal gene transfer that shows how an organism can acquire a complete, entirely functional gene, hundreds to thousands of nucleotides long, that can create a completely novel organism, occupying an entirely new niche, from an organism not even in that organisms domain, without human intervention, in nature.

In biological taxonomy, a domain is the highest taxonomic rank of organisms in the three-domain system. For example life is ordered into eight distinct classifications (domain, kingdom, phylum, class, order, family, genus, and species) and the higher you go in the rankings, the more unrelated the organisms are to one another. Therefore, organisms in different domains are the least related organisms.

For example, organisms in different domains have several notable differences. For instance, organisms in the domain Bacteria are all prokaryotic microorganisms, meaning they're all single-celled. Moreover, their cells have no nucleus. On the other hand, all life that has a nucleus, membrane-bound organelles, and are multicellular, are in the domain Eukarya.

When I read a study like the 'Contribution of Horizontal Gene Transfer to the Evolution of Saccharomyces cerevisiae' I like to break the study down into a null/alternative hypothesis format and then break down the experiment used to test the hypotheses into a logical framework. For example, I derived two hypotheses from the study on the 'Contribution of Horizontal Gene Transfer to the Evolution of Saccharomyces cerevisiae'

Null Hypothesis #1 is that horizontal gene transfer does not occur between prokaryotes and eukaryotes.

Alternative Hypothesis #1is that horizontal gene transfer occurs between prokaryotes and eukaryotes

Null Hypothesis #2 is that horizontal gene transfer between prokaryotes and eukaryotes has not contributed to the evolution of Eukaryotes.

Alternative Hypothesis #2 is that horizontal gene transfer between prokaryotes and eukaryotes has contributed to the evolution of eukaryotes

The experiment:

Other researchers in other studies cited by the researchers in this study found that the phylogeny of horizontally transferred genes is characteristically different from the species phylogeny.

Phylogeny is the evolution of a genetically related group of organisms as distinguished from the development of the individual organism. In simpler terms, researchers have found that horizontally transferred genes are different from vertically transferred genes, from parent to offspring.

The researchers employed a genome-wide comparative screen to determine the extent of horizontal gene transfer in two related species of Yeast, S. cerevisiae and A. gossypii lineages, and they found a possible horizontally transferred gene because it was in the S. cerevisiae lineage and it wasn't in the A.

gossypi lineage. The gene they found allows for the utilization of organic sulfur compounds in anaerobic environments. A gossypi has a similar gene but it only allows for the utilization of sulfur in aerobic environments. Therefore, the gene gave S. cerevisiae the selective advantage of being able to utilize sulfur in anaerobic environments and therefore contributed to its evolution.

The researcher's findings suggest the acquisition of the gene facilitated the exploitation of anaerobic environments other organism could not survive in and therefore a gene acquired from bacteria contributed to its evolution. Moreover, the only other organism with this gene are the bacteria (prokaryotes) K. lactis, K. waltii, and S. kluyveri which supports the argument that the gene was horizontally transferred from one of these species of bacteria. Furthermore, the gene has higher sequence identity to bacteria sulfatases than to any gene found in eukaryotes besides S. cerevisiae, corroborating the hypothesis that this gene was horizontally transferred from one of these species of bacteria. Moreover, among currently sequenced species, S. cerevisiae is the only eukaryotic organisms with a gene of this class. Therefore, horizontal transfer between prokaryotes and eukaryotes is clearly a mechanism for the acquisition of new genes in eukaryotic organisms.

The horizontally transferred gene most likely provided a selective benefit. This selective benefit requires a selective pressure. In
the case of the transfer of the DHOD gene, it optimized S. cerevisiae for anaerobic conditions which indicates that adaptation to anaerobic conditions and anaerobic environments has been an

important part of the evolution of S. cerevisiae. The researchers realized that there had to be a mechanism of DNA transfer requiring foreign DNA to enter a cell and they cited other studies where researchers discovered Bacterium-to-fungus conjugation and natural transformation as possible explanations for how DNA from a bacterium with this gene could be taken up by S. cerevisiae. Note that both mechanisms, conjugation and transformation, are also used in labs to create genetically modified organisms.

The study rejected the null hypothesis #1: Horizontal gene transfer does not occur between prokaryotes and eukaryotes. And the study accepted the alternative hypothesis #1 Horizontal gene transfer occurs between prokaryotes and eukaryotes

The Study rejected the null hypothesis #2:

Horizontal gene transfer between prokaryotes and eukaryotes has not contributed to the evolution of Eukaryotes. And the study accepted the alternative hypothesis #2: Horizontal gene transfer between prokaryotes and eukaryotes has contributed to the evolution of eukaryotes

Even with the discovery that genes have been transferred between organisms through horizontal gene transfer, Liberals still argue that GMO's are inherently unnatural. However, human directed genetic manipulation of food began with the domestication of plants and animals through artificial selection at about 10,500 to 10,100 BC[98] There has been almost no such thing as, "natural," food for thousands of years, with the only possible exceptions being venison hunted in the wild and edibles foraged for in the wilderness, such as, say, mushrooms and berries. Liberals call GM food, that has genes transferred between different species, "franken food," and they argue that genetically modified food has not been around long enough to know its adverse effects. But the first food human beings created by crossing species barriers was a cross between rye and wheat created in 1875[99] Crossing genes from one species to another species is nothing new.

Liberals claim that GM crops have adverse environmental impacts. However some GM crops need 37% less pesticides sprayed on them which benefits the environment[100] Reduced pesticide spraying has made a significant contribution to reducing greenhouse gas emissions by over 10 billion kg, equivalent to removing five million cars from the roadways[101]

Studies have shown some GM crops are not only not bad for the environment, they're better for the environment[102] For example, Some GM crops such as soybeans don't require tillage before a new crop is planted. A study by Uri et al. Found a correlation between conservation tillage practices and the adoption of GM crops. This is relevant to the environment because conservation tillage has fewer adverse environmental impacts than conventional tillage [103]

For example, reduced tillage and no-till practices can improve water quality by reducing the amounts of sediments and sediment-associated chemicals in runoff from farm fields into surface water. [104] Scientists have linked algal blooms in waterways to nutrient enrichment resulting from the chemicals used in fertilizers that are released from the soil through conventional tillage. Run off of the chemicals in fertilizer causes nutrient enrichment in marine environments ultimately leading to tainted drinking water supplies, and hypoxia, which is also known as oxygen depletion, and when oxygen is depleted in marine environments, it kills marine animals.[105] Some people even argue that the repression of GM crops by the environmental movement is the real problem causing environmental degradation, not GM crops and not only are GM crops not the cause of environmental degradation, they are a possible solution to environmental degradation.[105]

Liberals claim that for-profit GM food companies (notably Monsanto) are screwing farmers[106] However, Monsanto gave free license to farmers in developing countries for a genetically modified rice known as, "golden rice."[106] Golden Rice was created through genetic engineering to biosynthesize beta-carotene, a precursor of vitamin

A, in the edible parts of rice.[107] It was intended to produce a fortified food to be grown and consumed in areas with a shortage of dietary vitamin A ,[108] a deficiency which is estimated to kill 670,000 children under the age of 5 each year.[109] However left-wing groups like Greenpeace oppose the use of any patented genetically modified organisms in agriculture and they oppose the cultivation of golden rice, claiming it will open the door to more widespread use of GMOs[110] Greenpeace apposes golden rice, even though studies have found it poses no risk to human health, and multiple field tests have taken place with no adverse side-effects to participants.[108]

Liberals claim that GM food causes cancer when in reality foods can be genetically modified to reduce the chance of getting cancer. For example, The Department of Agriculture recently approved a potato that has been genetically engineered to have lower levels of acrylamide, a suspected human carcinogen that the vegetable can produce when it is cooked at high temperatures when it is used to make things like potato chips and french fries.

There's a lot of superstitious ignorance surrounding GMO's. If you believe GMO's are harmful, you might as well also believe a camera steals your soul when someone takes your picture because that's the same kind of baseless superstition that people who fear GMO's have. Not only is GM food not harmful to you or the environment, GM crops are better for the environment and often times GM food is not only not bad for you, it's better for you [87]

Chapter 4

THE STUPID THINGS LIBERALS BELIEVE, 'WHITE MALE PRIVILEGE.'

"I hate bigots because they don't believe the same things I do."

Liberals believe white people are, "privileged," [112] and they define White privilege as a combination of exclusive standards and opinions that are supported by Whites in a way that continually reinforces social distance between groups on the basis of power, access, advantage, majority status, control, choice, autonomy, authority, possessions, wealth, opportunity, materialistic acquisition, connection, access, preferential treatment, entitlement, and social standing [113]."

According to Peggy McIntosh in her paper, White Privilege, Unpacking the Invisible knapsack, whites in Western societies enjoy advantages that non-whites do not experience, as "an invisible package of unearned assets". It has been compared by Peggy

McIntosh to an invisible, weightless knapsack of assets and resources."[114]

However, since White privilege is invisible, it is not measurable. Since it is not measurable, it is not falsifiable. Since White privilege is not falsifiable, it is not scientific. A scientific theory has to be falsifiable in order to be scientific. Falsifiability or refutability of a [scientific] statement, hypothesis, or theory is the inherent possibility that it can be proven false. A statement is called falsifiable if it is possible to conceive of an observation or an argument which negates the statement in question. Since white privilege is invisible and unmeasurable it is not falsifiable, therefore; it is not scientific.

Liberals believe White people, "define the societal norm." Thus, "achievements by members of the privileged group are not viewed as meritorious and the result of individual effort, but rather, as the result of privilege." [115] In other words, liberals believe all the accomplishments of a white person, particularly white men, are the result of privilege, and are not the result of merit and effort. Liberals believe white males should be successful without even trying while simultaneously wanting white men to fail, because that is the only thing that fits with their, 'white male privilege,' narrative. Liberals scoff at the possibility that white males tend to be more successful because they have better principles, values, morals and ethics, such as say, taking responsibility for the consequences of their actions and choices, rather than blaming the consequences of their actions and choices on everyone but themselves. Liberals claim minorities and women are not as successful as white men because of, 'discrimination.' However, who blames the invisible unmeasurable force of white male privilege for their personal failings? Do white males blame white male privilege for their personal failing? Or do, liberal women and minorities blame white male privilege for their personal failings?

When you're a white male, not only are you responsible for your own bad choices, you're also responsible for the bad choices of women and minorities according to 'white male privilege'.

In 2009, the incarceration rate of black males was over six times higher than that of white males, with a rate of 4,749 per 100,000 US residents.[116][117][118] And a report by the Pew Hispanic Center, in 2007 found Latinos "accounted for 40% of all sentenced federal offenders-more than triple their share (13%) of the total U.S. adult population". [119] According to the US Department of Justice, blacks accounted for 52.5% of all homicide offenders from 1980 to 2008, with whites 45.3% and "Other" 2.2%. The offending rate for blacks was almost 8 times higher than that of whites. [120] [121]

Liberals blame the higher rate of incarceration of Hispanic and Black males on discrimination and there is evidence to suggest that Black and Hispanic males are given longer sentences than white males when they commit the same crimes. For example, A 2012 University of Michigan Law School study found that African Americans are given longer federal sentences even when factoring prior criminal records, and that African American jail sentences tend to be roughly 10% longer than the sentences given to white people for the same crimes.[122] The study found that Federal Prosecutors of African American and Hispanic defendants are almost twice as likely to push for mandatory minimum sentences, leading to longer sentences and disparities in incarceration rates for federal offenses.[122] However, The probability of arrest given the commission of a crime is higher for whites than it is for blacks. This suggests that blacks are disproportionately arrested for crimes because they commit them at higher rates, not because law enforcement practices result in racially biased arrest decisions.[123] In other words, when whites commit crimes they're more likely to be arrested for their crimes than they are to get away with them, which suggests that law enforcement does not go after black criminals with greater veracity than they do white criminals, accounting for the disparity of incarceration rates between Hispanic. Black, and White men, rather it's that Black and Hispanic men commit more crimes.

The majority of juvenile delinquents and adult prisoners grew up in female-headed households. The rate at which black children are born into unmarried homes in the U.S. has gone from a quarter to three quarters. 72 percent of African American children are fatherless. There are more black children living without biological fathers in the home than children who do. [124] On the other hand, white males tend to take responsibility for the consequences of their actions and choices more often. Therefore, White Males practice self-control more often and they tend to consider long-term consequences more often. For example, personally, I do not believe a few moments of fleeting pleasure are worth a lifetime of suffering to a child and it's been shown that fatherless children are much more likely to suffer physical abuse, including sexual abuse, because of the men their mothers bring home. [124] Moreover, it's not the fault of White Males if you are an African American and choose to have unprotected sex and as a result create an unplanned pregnancy. Having unprotected sex is a choice, and it's no secret that a possibility of that choice is an unplanned pregnancy.

Liberals blame the actions and choices of African Americans on the history of discrimination against African Americans in the United States. Liberals point to "the legacy of slavery" and Jim Crow, but back when blacks had to enter establishments through separate doors, about 85 percent of black children were born to *married* parents. Ironically, as integration increased, so did black out-of-wedlock pregnancies. [124]

Liberals believe White privilege gives White people, " passive advantages," which include, cultural affirmations of one's own worth; presumed greater social status; and freedom to move, buy, work, play, and speak freely." [125] But are minorities really prevented from doing any of these things? Are there laws today that prevent minorities from moving freely, and speaking freely based on their race. On the other hand, there are White people who have violated the unwritten laws of political correctness and have suffered consequences, such as being fired from their job. For example, Jeff Varner, a contestant on the show "Survivor," was fired from his job as a real estate agent in North Carolina as a result of outing a transgender contestant on that show.[126] Is that an example of being allowed to speak freely?

Cheryl Harris describes whiteness as a form of property, which confers privileges on its holders. In "Whiteness as Property," Harris writes,

---

"The wages of whiteness are available to all whites, regardless of class position — even to those whites who are without power, money, or influence. Whiteness, the characteristic that distinguishes them from blacks, serves as compensation even to those who lack material wealth."[125]

Therefore, liberals believe even the poorest white person is more privileged than the wealthiest African American. According to White privilege, a homeless white man is more privileged than a wealthy and famous African American actor or actress, such as, say, Denzel Washington, Morgan Freeman, or Halle Berry. It may sound ridiculous, but liberals really do believe a rich and famous African American actor or actress is less privileged than a homeless white person-which is ludicrous. Privilege exists, but it's not based on race. It's based on socioeconomic status? The privilege that exists in America, exists as a result of class, not race. If privilege is truly based on race then there should be evidence that wealthy minorities are being denied the same privileges that wealthy white people enjoy? Where is this evidence? On the other hand, while there is a correlation between Blacks, Hispanics and crime, the data implies a much stronger correlation between poverty and crime than it does crime and any racial group. [127] In other words, socioeconomic status is what confers privilege, not race.

Adam A. Powell, Nyla R. Branscombe, and Michael T. Schmitt say that people in the least successful white ethnic and cultural groups are often the ones that are disadvantaged the most from any affirmative action that attempts to take into account white privilege.[128] Therefore, unlike the "invisible" racism McIntosh imagines, affirmative action is real systematic institutionalized discrimination that gives some people preferential treatment based on their race and or gender and denies others that same preferential treatment based on their race and or gender. Martin Luther King JR said he dreamed of a day when people would be judged based on the content of their character and not based on the color of their skin but affirmative action judges people based on the color of their skin. You cannot simultaneously believe what Martin Luther King JR believed and also believe in affirmative action. In other words, you cannot believe that people should not be judged based on the color of their skin like Martin Luther King JR believed and also believe in affirmative action, that people should be judged based on the color of their skin. The two beliefs are incompatible. It has to be one or the other. It cannot be both.

Despite being unscientific, liberals claim it's a fact that white males are, "privileged," [112] and white male privilege is taught across the United States at liberal arts colleges, but how are white males privileged when white males are the only race and gender combination that have laws that actively discriminate against them today, affirmative action laws? If you're a white male and you're denied an opportunity based on your race and gender and someone else is given that opportunity based on their race and/or gender, then how is the race and gender combination denied the opportunity the "privileged," race and/or gender combination?

Isn't giving someone an opportunity based on their race and/or gender and denying another person that same opportunity based on their race and gender, racism and sexism? If affirmative action isn't sexist then why isn't there affirmative action for males in fields dominated by females, like elementary education, where 87% of the teachers are female? [129] If affirmative action isn't racist, then why isn't there affirmative action in the NBA, were 76 percent of the players were African American in 2015- while only 12.6% of the population in the United States was African American during the same period? [130]

Aren't affirmative action laws against the equal protection clause of the fourteenth amendment, the same equal protection clause that resulted in the end of segregation in the south in the 1960's?

The equal protection clause provides that no state shall deny to any person within its jurisdiction "the equal protection of the laws," but affirmative action laws give preferential treatment to some people based on their race and/or gender and they deny others that same preferential treatment based on their race and gender. Shouldn't affirmative action laws be unconstitutional? How are white males privileged when they're the only race and/or gender combination discriminated against via unconstitutional laws?

If minorities are under-privileged, then how do liberals explain Asian Americans? In 2015 Asian Americans had the highest educational attainment level and median household income of any racial demographic in the [United States] [131] [132]If minorities are under-privileged, how do liberals explain Asian Americans, a racial minority only comprising 5% of the population, yet having the highest household income of any racial demographic? If White People are, more "privileged," than any other race then how do liberals explain that in 2015 Asian American men were the highest earning racial group, earning 117% as much as white American men and Asian-American women earning 106% as much as white American women? [133] If minorities are inherently under-privileged, how do liberals explain that Asian Americans are no more likely than non-Hispanic whites to live in poverty?[133]

Asian Americans comprise just 5% of the entire U.S. population and as of 2011, Hispanics accounted for 16.7% of the national population[122 and African Americans comprised 12.6% of the United States population.[122] If white privilege is real and white people are privileged in the United States because they are a majority of the population then one would expect Asian Americans to be even more under-privileged because they comprise even less of the population than either Latinos or African

Americans. However Asian Americans are not underprivileged as one would expect if there was such a thing as, 'white privilege,' in the United States today. In fact, Starting in the first few years of the 2000 decade, Asian American earnings began exceeding all other racial groups for both men and women.[134] In 2008 Asian Americans had the highest median household income overall of any racial demographic.[135][136] In 2012, Asian Americans had the highest educational attainment level of any racial demographic. [135][136] In 2015, Asian American men and women were the highest earning racial group, earning 117% and 106% as much as white American men and white American women, respectfully.[137]

There is no doubt that African Americans and Latinos have faced a history of systematic institutionalized discrimination in the United States but are Latinos and African Americans under-privileged today and not Asian Americans because only Latinos and African Americans have faced a history of systematic institutionalized discrimination? According to the Naturalization Act of 1790, only, "free white persons," were permitted to naturalize as American citizens. So the naturalization Act of 1790 not only prevented Latinos and African Americans from naturalizing as American citizens, it also forbid Asian Americans from naturalizing as American citizens. Since Asian Americans were ineligible for citizenship, it prevented Asian immigrants from accessing a variety of rights, such as voting, just as it prevented Latino American and African Americans from voting rights.[138] So, it was not only African American and Hispanics that have faced a history of systematic institutionalized discrimination in the United States, it was also Asian Americans who faced that same history of systematic institutionalized discrimination.[138] Therefore, if a history of systematic institutionalized discrimination is the reason African Americans and Hispanics are under-privileged today then why aren't Asian Americans also under-privileged today? All three groups share a similar history of systematic institutionalized discrimination but Asian Americans are doing better than everyone, including White Americans? If white privilege is real, then this should not even be possible.

Despite being just 5% of the population and having a history of systematic institutionalized discrimination against them, Asian Americans taken collectively today are not under-privileged like liberals claim African Americans and Latinos are. Asian Americans are well represented in the professional sector and tend to earn higher wages. [139] Many Asian Americans have also come to occupy high positions at leading corporations including a number of Asian Americans being Chief Marketing Officers of corporations. [140]

So, why aren't Asian Americans under-privileged? Are Asian Americans just smarter? Several studies have found when Asian Adoptees are raised by white parents Asians have higher IQ's [141] [142] [143]. Studying different races of adoptees raised by white parents is relevant to studying a racial basis of inheritance for intelligence because the theory is, although they may be different races, they were all raised in similar environments, by the same race of parents.

Generally, Black people, White people, and East Asian people have different average IQ's. However the specific reasons for this remain controversial." [144] Three studies found when East Asian adoptees were raised by white parents East Asians had higher IQ's but a study examining these studies titled, "Racial IQ Differences among Transracial Adoptees: Fact or Artifact?," found that when East Asian, White, and Black adoptees were all raised in the same environment by white parents the difference in their IQ's was not statistically significant, which hints at a minimal role for genes in racial IQ differences.[144] Therefore, if Asians are inherently no smarter than other races then why have Asian Americans achieved more collectively than African Americans and Latinos? Why do Asian Americans achieve more academically and professionally than other minorities? If it's not genetic, it has to be environmental.

It's my theory that it is the belief in white privilege itself which leads to low achievement. It is the belief by African Americans and Latinos that they are inherently under-privileged and discriminated against which results in achieving less. Why take responsibility for the consequences of your actions and choices when there is someone to blame for your failures, like, say, White People and their privilege? Blaming other people for the consequences of your choices, for your actions, is not a successful life strategy for anyone, regardless of race. You're not going to be an asset to a company if you blame other people for the consequences of your actions, and choices. Taking responsibility and not blaming others is the foundation for success. It is a prerequisite for academic and professional achievement.

The mind is very powerful and can manifest things into reality that are not real, like white privilege. For example, some people with schizophrenia smell things as if those things are right in front of their face, but there is nothing there. It is all in their mind. You're not going to be likely to persevere through challenges if you believe there is some invisible and unmeasurable force working against you, stifling all of your efforts to overcome challenges and achieve more. It is the belief in white privilege that leads to low achievement. Believing in white privilege creates a self-fulfilling prophesy. Many African Americans and Latino's believe there is an invisible and unmeasurable force working against them when in reality there is little evidence of systematic institutionalized discrimination against Latinos or African Americans, today. Personal responsibility is the key to academic and professional success. It is the very cornerstone of achievement.

People who believe in White Privilege behave in astoundingly ridiculous ways. For example, Students at the University I graduated from had a day banning all white people from campus, (a ban which should be unconstitutional according to the 14th amendments equal protection clause) However, a white professor showed up anyway calling the ban, "an act of oppression," and he received death threats and he had to be escorted off campus by police. In this video, https://www.youtube.com/watch?v=l06t5njtt4o [145] posted on youtube students can be heard chanting black power while simultaneously calling white professors racist and the students were unable to comprehend the Irony of chanting a racist slogan, while simultaneously calling someone else, "racist." However, their actions do make sense in light of what is taught at liberal arts colleges in regards to white privilege. Students are taught that all white people are racist, whether, they know it or not, and African Americans are not capable of racism. Therefore, you can see how students taught white privilege can chant, "black power," and simultaneously call someone else racist and not comprehend how stupid that is. Many students come to universities with an inclination towards hating white males and by the time they graduate that inclination is often a rabid hatred of white males. It is the sexism and racism taught at these universities that creates that hatred.

There is no doubt that people have faced a history of systematic institutionalized discrimination. However, somehow Liberals believe white people, particularly white men, should be responsible for what other white people did hundreds of years ago before anyone alive today was born. This is a ridiculous notion. No one is responsible for what other people did before they were born. The only responsibility people have is the responsibility for their own personal actions and choices, not the actions and choices of people who were alive long before they were born. However, that doesn't stop Liberals from looking at white men the same way the Nazis looked at the Jews, as the scapegoats for everything.

Chapter 5

THE DUMB THING LIBERALS BELIEVE: MODERN FEMINISM IS AN EQUALITY MOVEMENT.

*"Ultimately, equality is in women's best interests, and women
will achieve more if they are equal"*

Liberals believe modern Feminism is an equality movement when in reality, modern Feminism more closely resembles a politically correct supremacist hate movement like the KKK in the South in the early twentieth century than it does an equality movement. That's why liberal's belief that Feminism is an equality movement is another really stupid thing liberal's believe.

If feminism is an equality movement, then shouldn't we hear feminists complaining about the sentencing gap at least as often as the wage gap? In a research paper by Sonja B. Starr titled, *Estimating Gender Disparities in Federal Criminal Cases,* she found when women are arrested for the same crimes as men they receive over a 60% reduced sentence and that's after being many times less likely to even be prosecuted in the first place after they have been arrested. [146] But you never hear Feminists complaining about the sentencing Gap like you do the wage gap because Feminism today is not about equality. Modern Feminism is about absolving women of what little accountability they do have. Equality would mean equal accountability and modern feminists are not working for equal accountability. If they were, they'd be working on the sentencing gap as enthusiastically as they do the wage gap.

Ultimately equality is in women's best interest. Women will achieve more if they are held as equally accountable as men for the consequences of their actions and choices. Only 18% of the worlds firms have a female as top chief executive officer and only 2% of the world's 500 biggest companies are headed by a female CEO. What accounts for these paltry numbers? Feminists claim it is discrimination.

However, disregard gender for a second and consider this thought experiment. Two candidates are applying for the same job. Let's call them person A and person B. Person A takes responsibility for the consequences of their actions and choices and person B doesn't. Which person is likely to get hired and succeed in a company, person A, who is accountable and takes responsibility for the consequences of their actions and choices or person B, who is not accountable and does not take responsibility for the consequences of their actions and choices? Clearly, the person who is accountable is more likely to be hired and succeed regardless of their gender. Therefore, the reason women tend to achieve less is not the result of discrimination. It is that women tend to have inferior values, morals, principles, and ethics.

For example, Feminists argue the sentencing gap is caused by white men, therefore; it's not their problem. However they also blame white men for the wage gap and they care a great deal about the wage gap. Why do they only care about the wage gap and not the sentencing gap when they believe the cause of each is the same, white men? If feminism is an equality movement then shouldn't Feminists care about the sentencing gap at least as much as the wage gap? I mean, the sentencing gap is over 60%, and the wage gap is 22%, and 60% is greater than 22%, right?

The reason Feminists don't care about the sentencing gap is because feminists only care about inequalities when they affect women. At best feminists don't care when an inequality affects men, and at their worst feminists look at inequalities affecting men as victories for women, such as the post-secondary achievement gap in education. How can a movement say it stands for equality when it looks at inequalities as victories?

This   video

https://www.youtube.com/watch?v=OUb9Yb2ucZI

[147] which can be seen on youtube shows dozens of feminists sexually and physically assaulting peaceful passive men as thousands of other feminists cheer them on. Is assaulting peaceful passive people something an equality movement does, or is sexually and physically assaulting peaceful passive people something a supremacist hate movement does?

In general, if a movement just promotes one gender or one race it is not an Equality movement. Take any movement that claims to be an equality movement and ask yourself, "does this movement promote equality for all races and all genders or does it only promote one gender or one race?" If the movement only promotes one gender or one race, it is not an equality movement. For example:

Black Lives Matter, is it an equality movement or does it just promote one race? Black Lives Matter only promotes one race, therefore it is not an equality movement.

The American Indian Movement, is it an equality movement or does it just promote one race? The American Indian Movement, only promotes one race, therefore; it is not an equality movement.

The Klu Klux Klan, is it an equality movement or does it just promote one race? The Klu Klux Klan only promotes one race, therefore; it is not an equality movement.

The Men's Rights Movement, is it an equality movement or does it just promote one gender? The Men's Rights Movement only promotes one gender, therefore; it is not an equality movement.

Feminism, is it an equality movement or does it just promote one gender? Feminism only promotes one gender, therefore; it is not an equality movement.

Equalitarianism, is it an equality movement or does it just promote one race or one gender? Equalitarianism promotes equality for everyone regardless of gender and race, therefore equalitarianism is an equality movement.

Therefore, out of all of these movements, Black Lives Matter, Equalitarianism, The American Indian Movement, The Klu Klux Klan, The Men's Rights Movement, and Feminism, Equalitarianism is the only movement that is truly an equality movement. So what is equalitarianism?

Equalitarians believe inequalities are wrong when those inequalities are the result of discrimination regardless of race and gender. Equalitarians don't believe in engineering equal outcomes. Equalitarians simply believe in equity. For example, when an inequality is the result of something other than discrimination, like biology or choice, Equalitarians do not believe it is wrong, they believe it just is. For instance, men tend to be stronger than women, therefore; men tend to be better at physically demanding jobs. This is an inequality that is the result of biology, not discrimination.

Therefore, equalitarians do not believe it is wrong. They believe it just is.

However, men are not always stronger than women and therefore more capable of doing physically demanding jobs. For example, two women recently passed the army's elite ranger training school, most men couldn't do that. As such, Equalitarians believe opportunities should be based on merit, regardless of gender and race.

A really good show that demonstrates that capability depends on the individual, not on race and/or gender is, 'Naked and Afraid', because there are tough women on that show and there are weak women on that show and there are tough men on that show and weak men on that show. Equalitarians believe that merit does not depend on gender. Equalitarians believe merit depends on the individual regardless of gender. On the other hand, Feminists believe women are not as capable as men and therefore need laws that benefit only women. So, which movement is the sexist movement? The movement that believes capability depends on the individual regardless of gender, or the movement that believes women are not as capable as men?

Equalitarians do not believe in manufacturing equal outcomes. Equalitarians simply believe that inequalities that are the result of discrimination should be changed and people should be judged based on their merit, not on their race and/or gender.

Ultimately, equality is in women's best interests, and women will achieve more if they are held accountable the way men are.

Chapter 6

THE STUPID THINGS
LIBERALS BELIEVE:
SUGAR IS BETTER FOR
YOU THAN ARTIFICIAL
SWEETENERS LIKE
ASPARTAME

Liberals believe dumb things because they believe completely in things in almost the complete absence of evidence in the presence of overwhelming contradictory evidence. For example, Alternative medicine, "health guru," Dr. Mercola and creator of "the world's most popular health newsletter," calls aspartame, " a chemical poison" and "By Far the Most Dangerous Substance added to most foods today." [148] However, The FDA has reviewed more than 100 toxicological and clinical studies confirming that aspartame is safe for the general population. [149] FDA officials describe aspartame as "one of the most thoroughly tested and studied food additives the agency has ever approved" and its safety as "clear cut"[150]

But the dangers of consuming sugar are well known and widely accepted: an increased risk of obesity, and suspected of, or fully implicated as a cause in the occurrence of diabetes, cardiovascular disease, dementia, macular degeneration, and tooth decay. [151, 152, 153] And the evidence supporting claims that Aspartame is dangerous have almost completely been debunked. Dr. Mercola claims the following illness can be triggered or worsened by aspartame: Brain tumors, multiple sclerosis, epilepsy, chronic fatigue syndrome, parkinson's disease, alzheimers, lymphoma, birth defects, fibromyalgia, mental retardation and even diabetes.[154] Dr. Mercola claims that aspartame ingestion results in the production of methanol, formaldehyde and formate, [which can be toxic] [154] which is factual. However, David Hattan current Acting Director of the Division of Health Effects Evaluation in the United States Food & Drug Administration (USFDA) Center for Food Safety and Applied Nutrition explains, "...in the gastrointestinal tract aspartame is hydrolyzed to one of its component materials, methanol, as well as the two amino acids, phenylalanine and aspartic acid. This methanol is taken up by the cells of the body and metabolized first to formaldehyde and then to formate. " Hatten goes on to explain,

---

"aspartame ingestion results in the production of methanol, formaldehyde and formate--substances that could be considered toxic at high doses. But the levels formed are modest, and substances such as methanol are found in higher amounts in common food products such as citrus juices and tomatoes.[155]

For example, according to The American Cancer Society, "In the body, aspartame is broken down into phenylalanine, aspartic acid, and methanol," and like Hatten, The American Cancer Society also says, "Methanol can be toxic in high amounts, but the amounts that result from the breakdown of aspartame is lower than with many "natural" foods. For example, drinking a liter of diet soda would lead to consumption of 55 milligrams (mg) of methanol, as compared to as much as 680 mg of methanol from a liter of fruit juice." Therefore, a liter of fruit juice contains about 12 times as much methanol as a can of diet soda with aspartame. [156] So, you'd think there would be even more people suffering from the diseases Dr. Mercola claims aspartame can trigger or worsen from consuming fruit juice, however; there is no evidence supporting such a claim.

Dr. Mercola's claim that aspartame can either trigger or worsen brain tumors has also been debunked. For example, one early study suggested that an increased rate of brain tumors in the US during the 1980s might have been related to aspartame use. However, according to the National Cancer Institute (NCI), the increase in brain tumor rates actually began back in the early 1970s, well before aspartame was in use. And most of the increase was seen in people age 70 and older, a group that was not exposed to the highest doses of aspartame. [156]

Moreover in a more recent study which according to The American Cancer Society is the largest study of this issue, researchers from the National Cancer Institute looked at cancer rates in more than 500,000 older adults. This study found that, compared to people who did not drink aspartame containing beverages, those who did drink them did not have an increased risk of lymphomas, leukemias, or brain tumors. [156]

Dr. Mercola claims Aspartame causes obesity [157] Mercola writes, "One of the most appalling, especially to those consuming artificially sweetened sugar-free and diet products in the hopes of losing weight, is their propensity to fuel weight gain," and he cites an article in the Yale Journal of Biology and Medicine which says, "Several large scale prospective cohort studies found positive correlation between artificial sweetener use and weight gain."[158]

However, do artificial sweeteners cause weight gain? It's been proven that Sugar provides a large amount of rapidly absorbable carbohydrates, leading to excessive energy intake, weight gain, and metabolic syndrome. [159,160,161] Would people be better off just using sugar rather than artificial sweeteners? Do artificial sweeteners, like sugar, also cause weight gain?

Dr. Mercola claims they do. Dr Mercola even cites a study by a team of Massachusetts General Hospital (MGH) investigators who even revealed a potential reason why artificial sweeteners like aspartame prevent, rather than promote, weight loss. [162]

The study Mercola cites found that mice fed aspartame-laced drinking water gained weight and developed symptoms of metabolic syndrome while mice not fed the artificial sweetener did not. The researchers revealed that phenylalanine, an aspartame breakdown product, blocks the activity of a gut enzyme called alkaline phosphatase (IAP). In a previous study, IAP was found to prevent the development of metabolic syndrome (and reduce symptoms in those with the condition) when fed to mice.[163] Richard Hodin, MD, of the MGH Department of Surgery, said in a press release:[164]

"We found that aspartame blocks a gut enzyme called intestinal alkaline phosphatase (IAP) that we previously showed can prevent obesity, diabetes and metabolic syndrome; so we think that aspartame might not work because, even as it is substituting for sugar, it blocks the beneficial aspects of IAP."

However, there was a study that found that an artificial sweetener caused bladder cancer in mice but later it was found that Bladder cancer associated with saccharin ingestion was found to be specific to rodent physiology[165] Similarly, chocolate is toxic to dogs and can cause renal failure however it is non-toxic to humans. Moreover, Mice in the study were fed either plain water or water infused with the equivalent amount of aspartame found in 2 to 3 1/2 cans of soda, along with a normal diet or a high-fat diet. Mice in the high-fat group that drank aspartame-infused water gained more weight than those eating the same diet without aspartame in their water. However, the amount of Aspartame in 3 ½ cans of soda consumed by a mouse weighing less than a pound is much greater as a percentage of body weight than the amount of Aspartame consumed in 3 ½ cans of soda by a human being weighing well over 100 pounds. Moreover, aspartame does contain calories, however; Aspartame is hundreds of times sweeter than sugar and, therefore; less of it has to be to be used to have the same amount of sweetness as sugar, so its calorie contribution is almost nothing when people consume reasonable amounts. For example, Web MD states, Artificial sweeteners, also called sugar substitutes, are compounds that offer the sweetness of sugar without the same calories. They are anywhere from 30 to 8,000 times sweeter than sugar and as a result, they have much fewer calories than foods made with table sugar (sucrose). Each gram of refined table sugar contains 4 calories, and even though artificial sweeteners can contain calories, so much less of them have to be used to have the same amount of sweetness as sugar, that their calorie contribution is negligible. [166] Therefore, the mice were consuming calories by ingesting the equivalent artificial sweetener in 3 ½ cans of soda, but much less so than if they were consuming sugar, but they were consuming calories.

Dr. Mercola also cites another study, the San Antonio Heart Study, which involved nearly 4,000 adults, which found drinkers of artificially sweetened beverages consistently had higher BMIs (body mass index) than non-drinkers[167]. But is there evidence of a cause and effect relationship between people who use artificial sweeteners and obesity or are heavier people just more likely to consume diet products containing aspartame than thin people?

According to a study cited by Dr. Mercola Research published in the Journal of the Academy of Nutrition and Dietetics revealed that people who drink diet beverages may end up compensating for their "saved" calories by eating more foods high in sugar, sodium and unhealthy fats.[168] Interestingly, when sugar was covertly switched to aspartame in a metabolic ward, a 25 percent immediate reduction in energy intake was achieved [169]. Conversely, knowingly ingesting aspartame was associated with increased overall energy intake, suggesting overcompensation for the expected caloric reduction [162]. Therefore, it's not the diet soda causing weight gain. It's people compensating for the calories they did not consume drinking diet soda by eating foods high in sugar, sodium, and unhealthy fats, which are the real culprits of their weight gain, not the diet soda.

According to a researcher cited by Dr Mercola, Ruopeng, a kinesiology and community health professor at the University of Illinois,[170]

"It may be that people who consume diet beverages feel justified in eating more, so they

reach for a muffin or a bag of chips … Or perhaps, in order to feel satisfied, they feel compelled to eat more of these high-calorie foods."

Therefore, diet drinks may not help people control their weight if they're not paying attention to the types of food they consume. Ruopeng writes:

"If people simply substitute diet beverages for sugar-sweetened beverages, it may not have the intended effect because they may just eat those calories rather than drink them," he said. "We therefore recommend that people carefully document their caloric intake from both beverages and discretionary foods because both of these add calories -- and possibly weight -- to the body."[164]

"Discretionary foods" are high-calorie, nutrient-poor foods that do not provide essential nutrients that the human body needs but may add variety. Foods such as cookies, ice cream, french fries and pastries fall under this category

In conclusion, it's not that diet products containing artificial sweeteners are contributing to weight gain. It's that people compensate for the calories they're not consuming in artificially sweetened food by consuming high calorie nutrient poor foods like cookies, ice cream, and potato chips. Artificial sweeteners are not the cause of weight gain. It's that people who are overweight to begin with tend to consume diet products containing artificial sweeteners. Therefore, there is a correlation between diet products containing artificial sweeteners and obesity, however; there is no cause and effect relationship between consuming artificial sweeteners and obesity.

The opponents of aspartame claim that aspartame is not natural and sugar is natural, however, sugar is not natural. Sugar was invented. Sugar is manufactured from sugar cane and sugar beets and goes through several processes to become the granulated sugar you buy. For example:

Firstly, the raw sugar goes through a process called, "affination," in which the raw sugar is mixed with a heavy syrup and centrifuged to wash away the outer coating of the raw sugar crystals. It is then "clarified," by the addition of phosphoric acid and calcium hydroxide that combine to precipitate calcium phosphate. The Calcium phosphate particles entrap some impurities and absorb others, and then float to the top of a tank, where they are skimmed off.

After any remaining solids are filtered out, the clarified syrup is decolorized by filtration through a bed of activated carbon or through an ion-exchange resin.

The purified syrup is then concentrated to supersaturation and repeatedly crystallized under vacuum to produce white refined sugar. The sugar crystals are then seperated from the, "mothor liquor," by centrifuging to produce the granulated sugar.

It is then dried in a hot rotary dryer, and then cool air is blowed through Centrifugal Blower/fan for several days in so-called, "conditioning silos".

Sugar must be handled with care as sugar dust explosions can occur. For example, in 2008 a sugar dust explosion in a Georgia refinery killed 13 people. How many natural foods do you know of that can explode and kill people?

Opponents of aspartame argue, "but isn't there sugar in fruit?" It is true there is sugar in fruit but the sugar in fruit is fructose, which is metabolized completely differently by the body than the sucrose in granulated sugar. For example, fructose has a glycemic index of 25, while sucrose has a glycemic index of 65. The glycemic index of a food is important because foods with a low glycemic index are digested and absorbed slowly which produces a gradual rise in blood sugar and insulin levels and they have proven benefits for health, like weight control because they help control apatite and delay hunger[169]

Chapter 7

THE STUPID THINGS LIBERALS BELIEVE: SMOKING MARIJUANA IS HEALTHY

"Smoking a bowl is not as healthy as eating a bowl of Spinach"

During last years state election season 25 states were enacting cannabis legislation, and according to Gallup polling data Sixty percent of Americans believe that the use of marijuana should be legal. Recreational cannabis was already legal in Washington, Colorado, Oregon, Alaska, and Washington DC, and after the elections four more states legalized marijuana use: California (2016), Maine (2016), Massachusetts (2016), and Nevada (2016). However, is cannabis legalization as good a thing as legalization advocates claim?

Legalization advocates claim marijuana is far less dangerous than alcohol or tobacco. Legalization advocates claim that modern research suggests that cannabis is a valuable aid in the treatment of a wide range of clinical applications. These include pain relief -- particularly of neuropathic pain (pain from nerve damage) -- nausea, spasticity, glaucoma, and movement disorders. Marijuana is also a powerful appetite stimulant, specifically for patients suffering from HIV, the AIDS wasting syndrome, or dementia. Legalization advocates site emerging research that suggests that marijuana's medicinal properties may protect the body against some types of malignant tumors and are neuroprotective. [171] However, is cannabis as benign and even beneficial as legalization advocates claim?

Is cannabis a neuroprotective? Does cannabis guard or protect against destructive or poisonous effects upon nerve tissue? A 2007 study in the Lancet titled "Cannabis use and risk of psychotic or affective health outcomes" [172] found that prospective epidemiological studies have consistently reported that use of cannabis increases the risk of schizophrenia-like psychosis. In 2012, a report by the Schizophrenia Commission titled, "The abandoned illness: a report by the Schizophrenia

Commission, Rethink Mental Illness," concluded that cannabis use is the most preventable risk factor for psychosis.[173] In a 2015 study, also in The Lancet, titled, "Proportion of patients in south London with first-episode psychosis attributable to use of high potency cannabis: a case-control study," found if you have a vulnerability to schizophrenia and you smoke [cannabis], it's likely to trigger an episode. Smoking cannabis is likely to advance the [disease]. When people with certain risky genes associated with psychosis smoke [cannabis] the risk of developing schizophrenia goes up sixfold. [174]

Legalization advocates claim the paranoia some people experience after using cannabis is the result of cannabis being illegal. However this does not explain the increase of emergency visits of people experiencing psychosis in states where cannabis has been legalized. For example, a retrospective study examining data from the US Healthcare Cost and Utilization Project (HCUP) showed that emergency department visits grew 50.4% between 2007 and 2012 in Colorado. [175] Why would emergency room visits increase in a state where marijuana has been legalized if the cause of marijuana induced psychosis is paranoia about using an illegal drug? Clearly, marijuana induced psychosis is the result of something other than paranoia about using an illegal drug if emergency room visits have increased 50.4% in a state where marijuana has been legalized.

Is marijuana far less dangerous than tobacco as legalization advocates claim? Legalization advocates cite statistics that claim 400,000 deaths are attributed to tobacco smoking each year. However, a study by the National Institute of Health titled," Cannabis Use and Risk of Lung Cancer: a case-control study," found, that 1 joint of cannabis [is] similar to about twenty cigarettes for risk of lung cancer. This study found," The risk of lung cancer increased 8% for each joint-year of cannabis smoking, after adjustment for confounding variables including cigarette smoking." [176] Clearly, smoking cannabis is not, far less dangerous than tobacco, as legalization advocates clam, if smoking one joint is the equivalent of smoking twenty cigarettes for risk of lung cancer.

Is marijuana far less dangerous than alcohol as legalization advocates claim? Legalization advocates cite statistics that show that 50,000 people die each year from alcohol poisoning. They claim by comparison, marijuana cannot cause death by overdose. Which is true, no one has ever died from an overdose of cannabis, however; roughly 10 percent of Washington state drivers involved in fatal car crashes between 2010 and 2014 tested positive for recent marijuana use, with the percentage of drivers who had used pot within hours of a crash doubling between 2013 and 2014, according to a study by the AAA Foundation for Traffic Safety. Even though, no one has ever died from an overdose of marijuana, clearly there are risks associated with cannabis similar to alcohol. Peter Kissinger, president and CEO of the AAA Foundation for Traffic Safety wrote "Washington serves as an eye-opening case study for what other states may experience with road safety after legalizing the drug." [177]

Medical cannabis has several potential beneficial effects. However, the use of cannabis as a medicine has not been rigorously scientifically tested, often due to production restrictions and other governmental regulations. At the very least, these government regulations should be removed so that cannabis can be studied for its potential beneficial effects and I believe cannabis should be decriminalized for both medical and recreational use. However, cannabis is not as benign and cannabis has not been proven to be as beneficial as legalization advocates claim.

Chapter 8

THE REALLY STUPID THINGS LIBERALS BELIEVE. THE WAGE GAP IS THE RESULT OF DISCRIMINATION

"Today, the average full-time working woman earns just 77 cents for every dollar a man earns...in 2014, that's an embarrassment.It is wrong."

–President Obama, remarks on equal pay for equal work, April 8, 2014

Liberals believe stupid things because they believe completely in things in the complete absence of evidence in the presence of overwhelming contradictory evidence, even, and The Wage Gap is an excellent example of this. That's why it's another one of the really stupid things Liberals believe.

Normally you'll always find these three statistics in every single study you read: a mean, a standard deviation, and a population parameter like confidence intervals. However, a study exists on the wage gap that's so good it doesn't have confidence intervals. Normally a study will calculate confidence intervals because they tell you how likely population statistics are within a certain margin of error of the sample you actually took based on that samples size. However this study was so inclusive there was no need to calculate population parameters like confidence intervals, because the sample in this study is the entire population. This study is that good. The study titled tiled "An analysis of the reasons for the disparity between the wages of men and women" was prepared for The United States Department of Labor Employment Standards Division in 2009 by the CONSAD research corporation.[178]

The 2009 study for the United States Department of Labor Employment Standards Division found that all but 5% of the 22% wage gap is explained by choices made by the genders and there's no evidence to suggest the remaining 5% is the result of discrimination. In fact evidence suggests the remaining 5% gap is the result of more choice namely the Researchers at CONSAD believe the 5% gap is the result of women choosing more compensation in the form of non-wage benefits but the Researchers at CONSAD couldn't quantify this factor because of the limitations of their model, namely multivariate regression analysis.

When there is a high R value (coefficient of correlation) between dependent variables in multivariate regression analysis the results can't be quantified because there is said to be collinearity. Basically, when there is collinearity, you can't tell what's influencing what. Is the dependent variable, benefits, being influencing by the independent variable, gender, or is the dependent variable being influenced by another dependent variable in the model? However, it's possible that the remaining 5% is the result of more choice that just couldn't be quantified statistically. In a forward to the CONSAD study Charles E. James, SR, Deputy Assistant Secretary For Federal Contract Compliance wrote:

"Although additional research in this area is clearly needed, this study leads to the unambiguous conclusion that the differences in the compensation of men and women are the result of a multitude of factors and that the raw wage gap should not be used as the basis to justify corrective action. Indeed, there may be nothing to correct. The differences in raw wages may be almost entirely the result of the individual choices being made by both male and female workers"

Even though it's almost been entirely proven that the wage gap is the result of choice, not discrimination, liberals insist on blaming the consequences of women's choices and actions on men. For example, Barack Obama also insinuated a 22% wage gap exists that's the result of discrimination in his 2013 and 2014 State of the union addresses. [180]

Some of the pay gap can be explained by what the genders tend to choose to study at university. For example, men are much more likely to study STEM (science technology engineering and math). For instance, in a paper by Andresse St. Rose titled "STEM Major Choice and the Gender Pay Gap" she found in 2007 women earned 17 percent of Bachelors degrees in engineering, compared to earning 79 percent of Bachelors degrees in education. In 2006 women earned only 20 percent of Bachelor degrees in physics, computer science, and engineering.[180] In a 2007 paper by Dey and Hill titled Behind the Gender Pay Gap they found STEM degrees tend to have higher salaries than their peers with degrees in other disciplines. For example, one year after graduation, an education major working full time earned, on average, about 60 percent as much as an engineering major working full time ($525 versus $851 per week)[181] Despite earning most of the degrees in post-secondary education women are choosing not to major in subjects that result in them being qualified for the lucrative careers men are more likely to be qualified for when they graduate, and according to Liberals this is men's fault? If liberals believe in equality then shouldn't they believe women should be equally accountable for the consequences of their actions and choices as men? Blaming men for the consequences of your actions and choices is not accountability.

For decades, liberals have claimed that discrimination blocks women from landing academic positions in STEM fields. However a paper published online by the National Academy of Sciences by Wendy M Williams and Stephen J. Cecil titled National Hiring experiments Reveal 2:1 Faculty Preference For Women on STEM Tenure Track found that in experiments with professors from 371 colleges and universities across the United States that science and engineering faculty actually preferred women two-to-one over identically qualified male candidates for assistant professor   positions.   [181]

If you're preferred 2:1, you're not being discriminated against. Some people might even suggest a 1:1 preference of identically qualified candidates would be equality and a 2:1 preference for women over identically qualified male candidates is actually an indication of discrimination against men, not women.

Bibliography

[1] Gross, N. & Simmons, S. (2007). The social and political views of American professors. Working paper

[2] Klein, D. B., & Stern, C. (2009). By the numbers: The ideological profile of professors. In R. Maranto, R.

[3] Rothman, S. & Lichter, S. R. (2008). The vanishing conservative: Is there a glass ceiling? In R. Maranto

[4] Nicholas Kristof, A Confession of Liberal Intolerance https://www.nytimes.com/2016/05/08/opinion/sunday/a-confession-of-liberal-intolerance.html?_r=0 Accessed 05/30/2017

[5] Barkow et al. 1992

[6] "instinct." Encyclopædia Britannica. Encyclopædia Britannica Online. Encyclopædia Britannica, 2011. Web. 18 February 2011

[7] Cosmides, L.; Tooby, J. (13 January 1997). "Evolutionary Psychology: A Primer". Center for Evolutionary Psychology. Retrieved 22 July 2016

[8] Schacter et al. 2007, pp. 26–27

[9] Brown, Donald E. (1991) Human Universals. New York: McGraw-Hill.

[10] Pinker, S. (2003). The blank slate. NY: Penguin

[11] Hertz, Rosanna (1 January 1995). "Review of Paradoxes of Gender". American Journal of Sociology.

[12] Wolfe, Alan (June 1994). New Republic;, Vol. 210 Issue 23, p27

[13] Lorber, Judith (2011). "Seeing Is Believing: Biology as Ideology," pp. 11-18 in The Gendered Society Reader

[14] Robin Marantz Henig, She always felt more boyish than girlish." National Geographic, "Gender Revolution," January 2017

[15] Torjesen PA, Sandnes L (Mar 2004). "Serum testosterone in women as measured by an automated immunoassay and a RIA". Clinical Chemistry.

[16] Southren AL, Gordon GG, Tochimoto S, Pinzon G, Lane DR, Stypulkowski W (May 1967). "Mean plasma concentration, metabolic clearance and basal plasma production rates of testosterone in normal young men and women using a constant infusion procedure: effect of time of day and plasma concentration on the metabolic clearance rate of testosterone". The Journal of Clinical Endocrinology and Metabolism

[17] Southren AL, Tochimoto S, Carmody NC, Isurugi K (Nov 1965). "Plasma production rates of testosterone in normal adult men and women and in patients with the syndrome of feminizing testes". The Journal of Clinical Endocrinology and Metabolism

[18] Kalat JW (2009). "Reproductive behaviors". Biological psychology. Belmont, Calif: Wadsworth, Cengage Learning

[19] Pinyerd B, Zipf WB (2005). "Puberty-timing is everything!". Journal of Pediatric Nursing

[20] Archer J (2006). "Testosterone and human aggression: an evaluation of the challenge hypothesis" Neuroscience and Biobehavioral Reviews

[21] The Mating Mind How sexual choice shaped the evolution of human nature, Geoffrey Miller

[22] Francie Diep *March 17, 2015) 8,000 Years Ago, 17 Women Reproduced for Every One Man https://psmag.com/8-000-years-ago-17-women-reproduced-for-every-one-man-6d41445ae73d#.vl6nbgfr9 Accessed 02/19/2017

[23] Robin Marantz Henig, She always felt more boyish than girlish." National Geographic, "Gender Revolution," January 2017

[24] Chip Brown, "Gender Revolution," National Geographic, January 2017[25] Andresse St. Rose 2010. "STEM major choice and the gender pay gap" On Campus with Women http://archive.aacu.org/ocww/volume3

[26] Stephen J. Cecil and Wendy M. Williams, "National Hiring Experiments Reveal 2:1 Faculty Preference For Women on STEM Tenure Track," Proceedings of the National Academy of Sciences, http://www.news.cornell.edu/stories/...ulty-positions

[27] Chip Brown, "Gender Revolution," National Geographic, January 2017

[28] Deary, Ian J.; Irwing, Paul; Der, Geoff; Bates, Timothy C. (2007). "Brother–sister differences in the g factor in intelligence: Analysis of full, opposite-sex siblings from the NLSY1979". Intelligence

[29] Wai, Jonathan; Cacchio, Megan; Putallaz, Martha; Makel, Matthew C. (2010). "Sex differences in the right tail of cognitive abilities: A 30year examination". Intelligence

[30] Lehrke, R. (1997). Sex linkage of intelligence: The X-Factor. NY: Praeger

[31] Lubinski, D.; Benbow, C. P. (2006). "Study of Mathematically Precocious Youth After 35 Years: Uncovering Antecedents for the Development of Math-Science Expertise". Perspectives on Psychological Science.

[32] Tina Roseburg, "American Girl," National Geographic, January 2017

[33] CONSAD Research Corporation 2009. "An Analysis of Reasons for the Disparity in Wages Between Men and Women" Prepared for The United States Department of Labor Employment Standards Administration Accessed August 23, 2015. http://www.consad.com/content/report...l%20Report.pdf

[34] Duarte, J.; Crawford J.; Stern J.; Haidt J.; Jussim L.; Tetlock E.; Political Diversity Will Improve Social Psychological Science; Retrieved, June 11, 2017 From http://the-good-news.storage.googleapis.com/assets/pdf/psychology-political-diversity.pdf

[35] Ceci, S. J., Peters, D., & Plotkin, J. (1985). Human subjects review, personal values, and the regulation of

social science research. American Psychologist

[36] Inbar, Y., & Lammers, J. (2012). Political diversity in social and personality psychology. Perspectives on

Psychological Science

[37] Abramowitz, S. I., Gomes, B., & Abramowitz, C. V. (1975). Publish or politic: Referee bias in

manuscript review. Journal of Applied Social Psychology

[38] Hardin, C. D., & Higgins, E. T. (1996). Shared reality: How social verification makes the subjective

[39] [39] Gorski D (16 November 2009). "Conflicts of interest in science-based medicine". Science-Based Medicine.

[40] Hahnemann S. (1883) The Homoeopathc Medical Doctrine or "Organ of the Healing Art"

[41] Countercultural Healing: A brief History of Alternavie Medicine in America, James Whorton, PBS, November 4, 2003,

[42] Nature Cures – The History of Alternative Medicine in America, James C. Whorton, Oxford University Press, 2002, "Archived copy

[43] The Rise and Rise of Complementary and Alternative Medicine: a Sociological Perspective, Ian D Coulter and Evan M Willis, Medical Journal of Australia, 2004; 180 (11): 587–89

[44]] The Alternative Fix, Frontline, Public Broadcasting System

[45] The New Age of Alternative Medicine. Why New Age Medicine is Catching On Claudia Wallis, Time Magazine

[46] New Age Medicine, Encyclopedia of New Age Beliefs; John Ankerberg, John Weldon, 1996, pp. 470–508

[47] Smith, T (1983). "Alternative medicine". British Medical Journal (Clinical research ed.). 287

[48] IOM Report 2005 Committee on the Use of Complementary and Alternative Medicine by the American Public Board on Health, Promotion and Disease Prevention, Institute of Medicine, US National Academies (2005) Complementary and Alternative Medicine in the United States; Washington DC; National Academy Press

[49] Angel, M et al (1998), "Alternative medicine-the risks of untested and unregulated   remedies" New England Journal of Medicine 339

[50]   https://nccih.nih.gov/health/integrative-health   Accessed 07/09/2017

[51] K. Linde, N. Clausius, G. Ramirez, et al., "Are the⬚ Clinical Effects of Homoeopathy Placebo Effects? A Meta-analysis of Placebo-Controlled Trials," Lancet, September 20, 1997

[52] The end of homoeopathy" The Lancet, Vol. 366 No. 9487 p⬚ 690. The Vol. 366 No. 9503 issue (Dec 27, 2005) and by 14 studies from 2003 to 2007

[53] $2.5 billion spent, no alternative cures found". Alternative Medicine. NBCNews.com. Associated Press. 2009-06-10.

[54] Is taxpayer money well spent or wasted on alternative-medicine research?, Susan Perry, 5-8-2012, MinnPost

[55]   http://public.oed.com/about/the-oed-and-oxford-dictionaries/ Accessed 07/29/2017

[56] Peirce, Charles Sanders (1908). A Neglected Argument for the Reality of God. 7. Wikisource. pp. 90–112. with added notes. Reprinted with previously unpublished part, Collected Papers v. 6, paragraphs 452–85, The Essential Peirce v. 2, pp. 434–50

[57] J. N. Hays (2005). "Epidemics and pandemics: their impacts on human history". ABC-CLIO. p.151

[58] Behbehani AM (1 December 1983). "The smallpox story: life and death of an old disease". Microbiol Rev. 47 (4): 455–509

[59] "Smallpox and Vaccinia". National Center for Biotechnology Information. Archived June 30, 2007, at the Wayback Machine.

[60] https://web.archive.org/web/20070921235036/http://www.who.int/mediacentre/factsheets/smallpox/en/ Accessed 07/30/2017

[61] https://web.archive.org/web/20090628230753/http://jennermuseum.com/sv/smallpox2.shtml Accessed 07/30/2017

[62] Hopkins, Donald R. (2002). The greatest killer: smallpox in history, with a new introduction. Chicago: University of Chicago Press. p. 80

[63] J. N. Hays (2009). "The Burdens of Disease: Epidemics and Human Response in Western History". p. 126. Rutgers University Press J. N. Hays (2009). "The Burdens of Disease: Epidemics and Human Response in Western History". p. 126. Rutgers University Press

[64] Hahnemann, Samuel (1833). The homœopathic medical doctrine, or "Organon of the healing art". Dublin: W. F. Wakeman

[65] http://articles.mercola.com/sites/articles/archive/2008/07/24/ever-wonder-why-homeopathy-works.aspx Accessed 08/03/2017

[66] https://www.quackwatch.org/01QuackeryRelatedTopics/electro.html Accessed 08/02/2017

[67] Lewis GT and others. Is electrodermal testing as effective as skin prick tests for diagnosing allergies? A double blind, randomised block design study. British Journal of Medicine 322:131-134, 2001

[68] Katalaris CH and others. Vega testing in the diagnosis of allergic conditions. Medical Journal of Australia 155:113-114, 1991

[69] Countercultural Healing: A brief History of Alternavie Medicine in America, James Whorton, PBS, November 4, 2003

[70] Ernst, E. (2002). "A systematic review of systematic reviews of homeopathy". British Journal of Clinical Pharmacology. 54 (6): 577–82.

[71] House of Commons: Science and Technology Committee (22 February 2010). Evidence Check 2: Homeopathy (PDF) (Report). HC 45, Fourth Report of Session 2009–2010. London: The Stationery Office.

[72] Shang, Aijing; Huwiler-Müntener, Karin; Nartey, Linda; Jüni, Peter; Dörig, Stephan; Sterne, Jonathan AC; Pewsner, Daniel; Egger, Matthias (2005), "Are the clinical effects of homoeopathy placebo effects? Comparative study of placebo-controlled trials of homoeopathy and allopathy", The Lancet, 366 (9487): 726–732

[73] "Homeopathy: An Introduction". Backgrounders. NCCIH. 2013 [2009].

[74] Tuomela, R (1987). "Chapter 4: Science, Protoscience, and Pseudoscience". In Pitt JC, Marcello P. Rational Changes in Science: Essays on Scientific Reasoning. Boston Studies in the Philosophy of Science. 98. Springer. pp. 83–101

[75] Smith K (2012). "Homeopathy is Unscientific and Unethical". Bioethics. 26 (9): 508–512

[76] Baran GR, Kiana MF, Samuel SP (2014). Chapter 2: Science, Pseudoscience, and Not Science: How Do They Differ?. Healthcare and Biomedical Technology in the 21st Century. Springer. pp. 19–57

[77] Ladyman J (2013). "Chapter 3: Towards a Demarcation of Science from Pseudoscience". In Pigliucci M, Boudry M. Philosophy of Pseudoscience: Reconsidering the Demarcation Problem. University of Chicago Press. pp. 48–49

[78] National Science Board (2002). "Chapter 7: Science and Technology: Public Attitudes and Public Understanding, Section: Belief in Alternative Medicine". Science and Engineering Indicators - 2002. Arlington, Virginia: Division of Science Resources Statistics, National Science Foundation, US Government.

[79] Sampson, W. (1995). "Antiscience Trends in the Rise of the "Alternative Medicine" Movement". Annals of the New York Academy of Sciences. 775 (1): 188–197.

[80] Kent, H. (1997). "Ignore growing patient interest in alternative medicine at your peril - MDs warned". Canadian Medical Association Journal. 157 (10): 1427–8.

[81] Goldrosen, M.H.; et al. (2004). "Complementary and alternative medicine: assessing the evidence for immunological benefits". Perspective. Nature Reviews Immunology. 4 (11): 912–21.

[82] Goldrosen, M.H.; et al. (2004). "Complementary and alternative medicine: assessing the evidence for immunological benefits". Perspective. Nature Reviews Immunology. 4 (11): 912–21.

[83] Eisenberg, D.M.; et al. (1998). "Trends in alternative medicine use in the United States, 1990–1997: Results of a follow-up national survey". JAMA. 280 (18): 1569–75

[84] Kloor, Keith GMO Opponents Are the Climate Skeptics of the Left Slate

[85] http://blogs.discovermagazine.com/collideascape/2012/10/19/liberals-turn-a-blind-eye-to-crazy-talk-on-gmos/#.Uueb32Qo5GG

[86] Robinson, K. M., Sieber, K. B., & Dunning Hotopp, J. C. (October 2013). "A review of bacteria-animal lateral gene transfer

may inform our understanding of diseases like cancer". PLoS Genet. 9 (10)

[87] World Health Organization. Food safety: 20 questions on genetically modified foods. Accessed December 22, 2012

[88] American Association for the Advancement of Science (AAAS), Board of Directors (2012). Statement by the AAAS Board of Directors On Labeling of Genetically Modified Foods, and associated Press release: Legally Mandating GM Food Labels Could Mislead and Falsely Alarm Consumers

[89] American Medical Association (2012). Report 2 of the Council on Science and Public Health: Labeling of Bioengineered Foods

[90] World Health Organization. Food safety: 20 questions on genetically modified foods. Accessed December 22, 2012

[91] ^ United States Institute of Medicine and National Research Council (2004). Safety of Genetically Engineered Foods: Approaches to Assessing Unintended Health Effects. National Academies Press. Free full-text. See pp11ff on need for better standards and tools to evaluate GM food.

[92] A decade of EU-funded GMO research (2001-2010) (PDF). Directorate-General for Research and Innovation. Biotechnologies, Agriculture, Food. European Union. 2010. p. 16. doi:10.2777/97784. ISBN 978-92-79-16344-9.

[93] Ochman, H., Lawrence, J. G., & Groisman, E. A. (May 2000). "Lateral gene transfer and the nature of bacterial innovation

[94] Dunning Hotopp, J. C. (April 2011). "Horizontal gene transfer between bacteria and animals". Trends in Genetics

[95] Syvanen M (January 1985). "Cross-species gene transfer; implications for a new theory of evolution" (PDF). J. Theor. Biol

[96] Stearns, S. C., & Hoekstra, R. F. (2005). Evolution: An introduction (2nd ed.). Oxford, NY: Oxford Univ. Press[97] Hall C, Brachat S, Dietrich FS (June 2005). "Contribution of Horizontal Gene Transfer to the Evolution of Saccharomyces cerevisiae". Eukaryotic Cell[98] Daniel Zohary, Maria Hopf, Ehud Weiss (2012). Domestication of Plants in the Old World: The origin and spread of plants in the old world. Oxford University Press[99]] Klümper W, Qaim M (2014) A Meta-Analysis of the Impacts of Genetically Modified Crops. PLoS ONE 9(11): e111629. doi:10.1371/journal.pone.0111629

[100] Graham Brookes and Peter Barfoot, "GM Crops: The Global Economic and Environmental Impact - The First Nine Years 1996-2004" The Journal of Agrobiotechnology Management & Economics, Volume 8 // Number 2 & 3 // Article 15

[101] [205] Abud S. et al., "Impact of Genetically Engineered Crops on Farm Sustainability in the United States" The National Academies Press, 2010

[102] Chislock, M. F., Doster, E., Zitomer, R. A. & Wilson, A. E. (2013) Eutrophication: Causes, The Nature Education Knowledge Project, Accessed February 12th 2016[103] Dick Taverne "The real GM food scandal ," Prospect Magazine, November 25, 2007

[104] Amy Harmon for The New York Times, Jan 4, 2014. A Lonely Quest for Facts on Genetically Modified Crops

[105] http://www.nature.com/scitable/knowledge/library/eutrophication-

causes-consequences-and-controls-in-aquatic-102364466   Accessed 08/ 06/ 2015

[106] Ye, X; Al-Babili, S; Klöti, A; Zhang, J; Lucca, P; Beyer, P; Potrykus, I (2000). "Engineering the provitamin A (beta-carotene) biosynthetic pathway into (carotenoid-free) rice endosperm". Science 287 (5451): 303–5. doi:10.1126/science.287.5451.303. PMID 10634784

[107] Ye, X; Al-Babili, S; Klöti, A; Zhang, J; Lucca, P; Beyer, P; Potrykus, I (2000). "Engineering the provitamin A (beta-carotene) biosynthetic pathway into (carotenoid-free) rice endosperm". Science 287 (5451): 303–5. doi:10.1126/science.287.5451.303. PMID 10634784

[108] One existing crop, genetically engineered "golden rice" that produces vitamin A, already holds enormous promise for reducing blindness and dwarfism that result from a vitamin-A deficient diet. - Bill Frist, physician and politician, in a Washington Times commentary - November 21, 2006

[109] Black RE et al., Maternal and child undernutrition: global and regional exposures and health consequences, The Lancet, 2008, 371(9608), p. 253.

[110]   Genetic   Engineering".   Greenpeace. "Golden Rice: All glitter, no gold". Greenpeace. March 16, 2005.

[111] One existing crop, genetically engineered "golden rice" that produces vitamin A, already holds enormous promise for reducing blindness and dwarfism that result from a vitamin-A deficient diet. - Bill Frist, physician and politician, in a Washington Times commentary - November 21, 2006

[112] "An Open Letter to White Men in America," Huffpost Religion, Accessed February, 21, 2016, http://www.huffingtonpost.com/rev-dr-john-c-dorhauer/an-open-letter-to-white-m_b_7857790.html

[113] (Hays & Chang, 2003; Manning & Baruth, 2009)

[114] McIntosh, Peggy. "White privilege: Unpacking the Invisible Knapsack" (PDF). Independent School, Winter90, Vol. 49 Issue 2, p31, 5p

[115] Marwit, Samuel J.; Walker, Elaine F.; Marwit, Karen L. (December 1977). "Reliability of Standard English Differences among Black and White Children at Second, Fourth, and Seventh Grades". Child Development. Blackwell Publishing on behalf of the Society for Research in Child Development. 48 (4): 1739–42.

[116] "Number of State Prisoners Declined By Almost 3,000 During 2009; Federal Prison Population Increased By 6,800

[117] Kouzmin, Alexander (2012). State Crimes Against Democracy: Political Forensics in Public Affairs

[118] Prison Inmates at Midyear 2009 - Statistical Tables - US Bureau of Justice Statistics, published June 2010. See tables 16-19 for totals and rates for blacks, Hispanics, and whites. Broken down by year, gender, and age. See page 2 for "Selected characteristics of inmates held in custody in state or federal prisons or in local jails". It has the overall incarceration rate.

119] Handbook of Crime Correlates; Lee Ellis, Kevin M. Beaver, John Wright; 2009; Academic Press

[120] "Homicide Trends in the United States, 1980-2008"

[121] Cooper, Alexia (2012). Homicide Trends in the United States, 1980-2008

[122] Rehavi and Starr (2012) "Racial Disparity in Federal Criminal Charging and Its Sentencing Consequences" rkWoing Paper Series, no. 12-002 (Univ. of Michigan Law & Economics, Empirical Legal Studies Center

[123] D'Alessio, S. J.; Stolzenberg, L. (1 June 2003). "Race and the Probability of Arrest". Social Forces.j

[124] '72 Percent' Documentary on Fatherless Black Children Black Community News https://blackcommunitynews.com/72-percent-documentary-on-fatherless-black-children/ Accessed 07/02/2017

[125]] Cheryl, Harris (1995). "Whiteness as Property". In Crenshaw, Kimberlé. Critical Race Theory: The Key Writings that Formed the Movement. New York: The New Press. p. 286.

[126] Variety, 'Survivor' Contestant Fired From Job After Transgender Outing Controversy' http://variety.com/2017/tv/news/survivor-transgender-outing-jeff-varner-fired-zeke-smith-1202031498/ Accessed 06/26/ 2017

[127] Handbook of Crime Correlates; Lee Ellis, Kevin M. Beaver, John Wright; 2009; Academic Press

[128] Ref name="Privilege">Blum, Lawrence. "'White Privilege': A Mild Critique1." Theory and Research in Education. 2008. 6:309

[129] "Percentage of teachers in primary education who are female," The World Bank, Accessed February 21, 2016, http://data.worldbank.org/indicator/SE.PRM.TCHR.FE.ZS

[130] "An all black basketball league," American Thinker, Accessed February 21, 2016, http://www.americanthinker.com/articles/2014/04/an_all_black_bas ketball_league.html

[131] "Educational Attainment in the United States: 2007" (PDF). U.S. Census Bureau. 2009.

[132] "Income, Poverty, and Health Insurance Coverage in the United States: 2008" (PDF). U.S. Census Bureau. 2009. p. 9.

[133] Takei, Isao; Sakamoto, Arthur (2011-01-01). "Poverty among Asian Americans in the 21st Century". Sociological Perspectives

[134] US Census Bureau Public Information Office. "Most Children Younger Than Age 1 are Minorities, Census Bureau Reports - Population - Newsroom - U.S. Census Bureau

[135] "Educational Attainment in the United States: 2007" (PDF). U.S. Census Bureau. 2009.

[136] "Income, Poverty, and Health Insurance Coverage in the United States: 2008" (PDF). U.S. Census Bureau. 2009. p. 9.

[137] Patten, Eileen. "Racial, gender wage gaps persist in U.S. despite some progress"

[138] Amazon.com: Impossible Subjects: Illegal Aliens and the Making of Modern America (Politics and Society in Twentieth-Century America) eBook: Mae M. Ngai: Books". www.amazon.com. Retrieved February 21, 2016.

[139] Broad racial disparities persist". Archived from the original on November 30, 2006. Retrieved December 18, 2006.

[140] "Notable Asian American Professionals"

[141] Rushton, J.P.; Jensen, A.R. Race and IQ: A Theory-Based Review of the Research in Richard Nisbett's Intelligence and How to Get It. Open Psychol. J. 2010, 3, 9–35. [Google Scholar] [CrossRef]

[142] Lynn, R. Some Reinterpretations of the Minnesota Transracial Adoption Study. Intelligence 1994, 19, 21–27. [Google Scholar] [CrossRef]

[143] Rushton, J.P.; Jensen, A.R. Thirty years of research on race differences in cognitive ability. Psychol. Public Policy Law 2005, 11, 235–294. [Google Scholar] [CrossRef]

[144] Thomas, D. Racial IQ Differences among Transracial Adoptees: Fact or Artifact? J. Intell. 2017, 5, 1.

[145] https://www.youtube.com/watch?v=l06t5njtt4o

[146] Sonja B. Starr 2012. "Estimating Gender Disparities in Federal Criminal Cases" University of Michigan Law and Economics Research Paper Accessed August 23, 2015 http://papers.ssrn.com/sol3/papers.cfm?abstract_id=2144002

[147] https://www.youtube.com/watch?v=OUb9Yb2ucZl

[148] http://articles.mercola.com/sites/articles/archive/2011/11/06/aspartame-most-dangerous-substance-added-to-food.aspx Retrieved December 6th 2016

[149] https://web.archive.org/web/20090120185049/http://www.fda.gov/FDAC/features/1999/699_sugar.html Accessed December 6th 2016

[150] Henkel, John (November–December 1999). "Sugar Substitutes: Americans Opt for Sweetness and Lite". FDA Consumer. DIANE Publishing. 33 (6): 12–6. ISBN 978-1-4223-2690-9. PMID 10628311. Archived from the original on 16 November 2008. Retrieved 29 January 2009

[151] Popkin BM, Nielsen SJ. The sweetening of the world's diet. Obes Res. 2003;11:1325–1332[152] Schulze MB, Manson JE, Ludwig DS, Colditz GA, Stampfer MJ, Willett WC. et al. Sugar-sweetened beverages, weight gain, and incidence of type 2 diabetes in young and middle-aged women. JAMA. 2004;292:927–934

[153] Saris WHM. Sugars, energy metabolism, and body weight control. Am J Clin Nutr. 2003;78:850S–857S

[154] http://articles.mercola.com/sites/articles/archive/2011/11/06/aspartame-most-dangerous-substance-added-to-food.aspx Retrieved December 6th 2016

[155] https://www.chem.purdue.edu/courses/chm333/Spring%202012/Handouts/Aspartame%20Controversy.pdf Accessed December 6th 2016

[156] www.cancer.org/cancer/cancercauses/othercarcinogens/athome/aspartame Accessed December 6th 2016

[157] http://articles.mercola.com/sites/articles/archive/2016/12/06/aspartame-causes-obesity.aspx accessed 12/22/2016

[158]] Yale J Biol Med. 2010 Jun; 83(2): 101–108.

[159] Popkin BM, Nielsen SJ. The sweetening of the world's diet. Obes Res. 2003;11:1325–1332[160] Schulze MB, Manson JE, Ludwig DS, Colditz GA, Stampfer MJ, Willett WC. et al. Sugar-sweetened beverages, weight gain, and incidence of type 2 diabetes in young and middle-aged women. JAMA. 2004;292:927–934

[161] Saris WHM. Sugars, energy metabolism, and body weight control. Am J Clin Nutr. 2003;78:850S–857S.[162] Applied Physiology, Nutrition, and Metabolism November 18, 2016[163] Preventive Medicine 1986 Mar;15(2):195-202

[164] EurekAlert November 22, 2016[165] Kroger M, Meister K, Kava R. Low-calorie Sweeteners and Other Sugar Substitutes: A

Review of the Safety Issues. Comprehensive Reviews in Food Science and Food Safety. 2006;5:35–47[166] http://www.webmd.com/food-recipes/features/are-artificial-sweeteners-safe#1 Accessed 12/20/2016[167] Obesity (Silver Spring). 2008 Aug;16(8):1894-900. [168] Preventive Medicine 1986 Mar;15(2):195-202 [169] Kroger M, Meister K, Kava R. Low-calorie Sweeteners and Other Sugar Substitutes: A Review of the Safety Issues. Comprehensive Reviews in Food Science and Food Safety. 2006;5:35–47[169] Journal of the Academy of Nutrition and Dietetics September 9, 2015

[170] Porikos KP, Booth G, Van Itallie TB. Effect of covert nutritive dilution on the spontaneous food intake of obese individuals: a pilot study. Am J Clin Nutr. 1977;30:1638–1644

[171] http://norml.org/ Accessed 03/06/2016

California (2016), Maine (2016), Massachusetts (2016), and Nevada (2016).

[172] Moore TH[1], Zammit S, Lingford-Hughes A, Barnes TR, Jones PB, Burke M, Lewis G. (2007) "Cannabis use and risk of psychotic or affective health outcomes" https://www.ncbi.nlm.nih.gov/pubmed/17662880 Accessed 03/16/2017

[173] https://www.rethink.org/about-us/the-schizophrenia-commission Accessed 03/07/2016

[174] Marta Di Forti, et al "Proportion of patients in south London with first-episode psychosis attributable to use of high potency cannabis: a case-control study" http://www.thelancet.com/pb/assets/raw/Lancet/pdfs/14TLP0454_D i%20Forti.pdf Accessed 03/14/2016

[175] Deborah Brauser (12/16/2014), "Cannabis-Related ED Visits Rise in States With Legalized Use" Medscape, http://www.medscape.com/viewarticle/836663 Accessed 03/ 12/ 2016

[176] Sarah Aldington,[1] Matire Harwood,[1] Brian Cox,[2] Mark Weatherall,[3] Lutz Beckert,[1] Anna Hansell,[4] Alison Pritchard,[1] Geoffrey Robinson,[1] and Richard Beasley[1,5] CANNABIS USE AND RISK OF LUNG CANCER: A CASE-CONTROL STUDY (08/14/2008) NCBI https://www.ncbi.nlm.nih.gov/pmc/articles/PMC2516340/ Accessed 03/16/2016

[177] Andrea Noble, (05/10/2016) TheWashington Times, "Marijuana-related fatal car accidents surge in Washington state after legalization, http://www.washingtontimes.com/news/2016/may/10/marijuana-related-fatal-car-accidents-surge-washin/ Accessed 03/12/2016

[178] CONSAD Research Corporation 2009. "An Analysis of Reasons for the Disparity in Wages Between Men and Women" Prepared for The United States Department of Labor Employment Standards Administration Accessed August 23, 2015. http://www.consad.com/content/report...l%20Report.pdf

[179] Glenn Kessler," President Obama's persistent '77-cent' claim on the wage gap gets a new Pinocchio rating," The Washington

[180] Dey, J. G., and C. Hill. 2007. Behind the pay gap. Washington, DC: AAUW Educational Foundation National Association of Colleges and Employers. 2009. Salary survey

[181] Dey, J. G., and C. Hill. 2007. Behind the pay gap. Washington, DC: AAUW Educational Foundation

National Association of Colleges and Employers. 2009. Salary survey